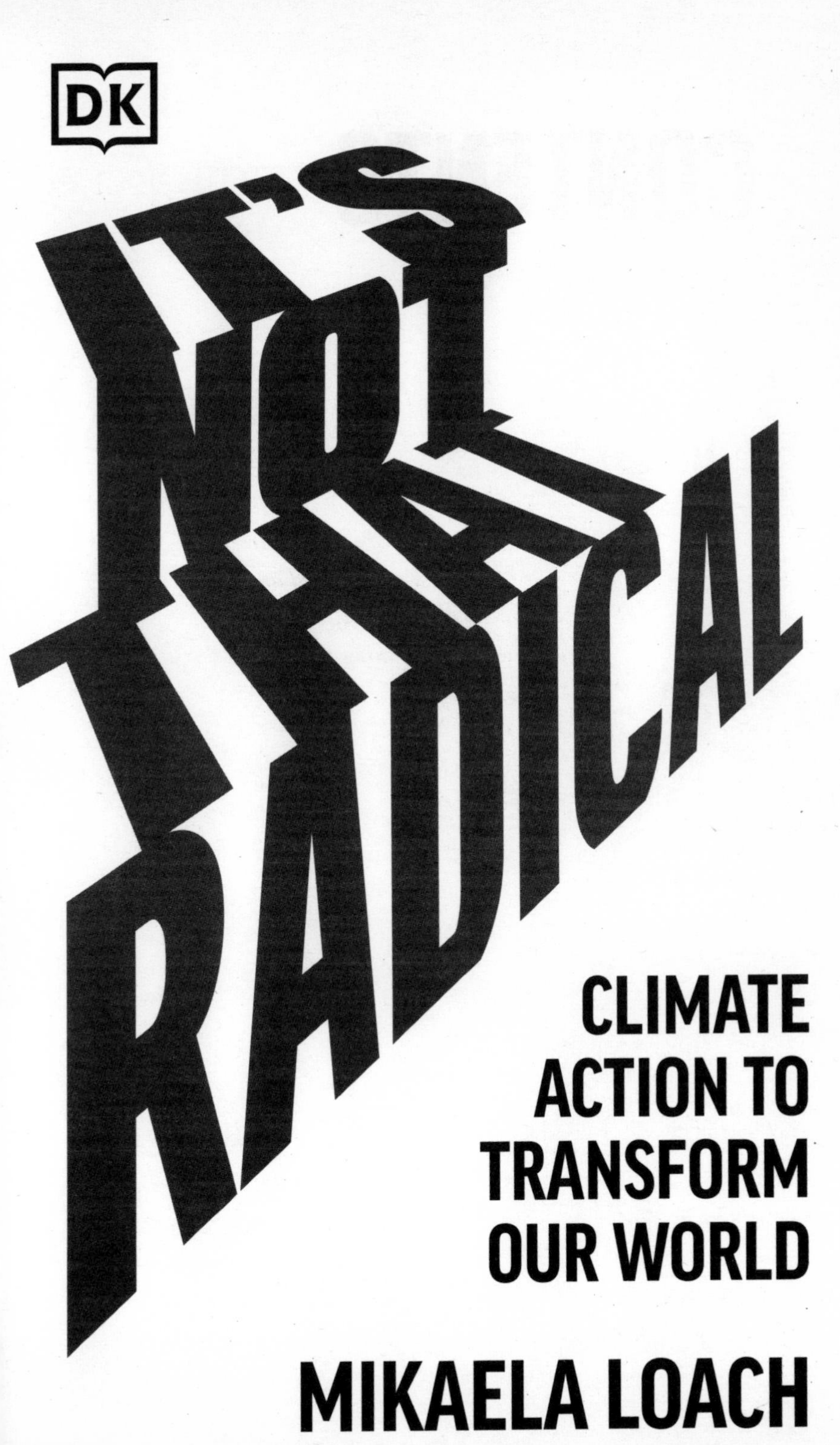

CLIMATE
ACTION TO
TRANSFORM
OUR WORLD

MIKAELA LOACH

CONTENTS

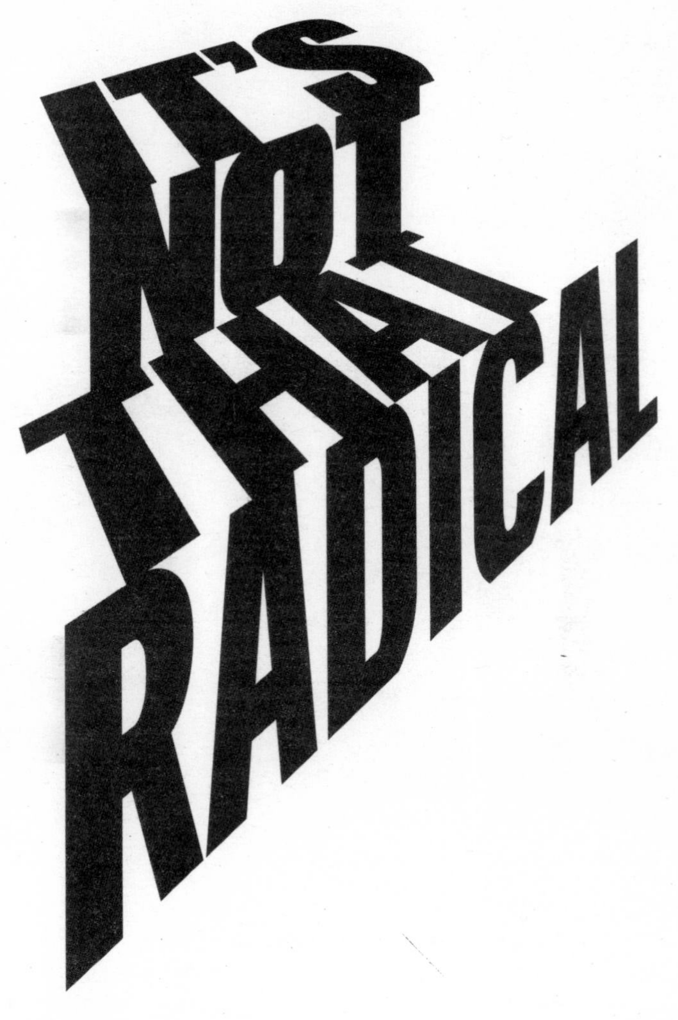
IT'S
NOT
THAT
RADICAL

To all the ancestors who gave their lives to building a transformed and liberated world for us all. May we honour them by continuing that fight.

INTRODUCTION

This is a book for anyone who has ever felt doom, anxiety or powerlessness in the face of the climate crisis. If you've ever felt that the current situation is too big or too complicated for you to understand or even begin to tackle, then this book is for you. This is not a defeatist book. It's not a book about giving up. This is a book that will transform any feelings of anxiety, fear or overwhelm into action. It is about transforming our entire world for the better. It is a book about active hope; about all that is possible once we let go of the baggage of the old world and have the bravery to step into – and build – a new one. We urgently need to reframe our understanding of the climate crisis and the systems that caused it, in order to transform the world for the better. This is the most important challenge and significant opportunity that humanity has ever faced.

A huge part of the anxiety we feel about the climate crisis comes from this feeling that it's something insurmountable; that it's too far out of our hands; that we are powerless to do anything about it, and that we're alone in feeling like this. Through taking action, through organising and campaigning, I've come to realise that we aren't powerless at all. We aren't alone. I've seen first-hand how everything can change when we come together, form movements and refuse to accept that the world will always be this way. We can find a community that can hold us when we need to be held, and stand beside us in action.

Fear has dominated the narratives around climate. All too often, the focus is either catastrophic and doom-laden, or else filled with delusional ideas that we can afford to wait or not do anything at all. No wonder you might not have wanted to pick up this book – almost every other story we have been told about climate has led people to either be overwhelmed or to catastrophise. I don't believe that fear is a great motivator; rather, it's a great divider. It doesn't lead to actions rooted in justice, but instead, ones rooted in panic. If we continue on this path, we will be condemned to disaster. Thankfully, there is another way.

The undeniable truth is that the climate crisis is the biggest issue facing us all collectively. But that doesn't require us to leave our hopes, dreams, desires or struggles at the door in order to fight for this cause. The fact that the climate crisis is inherently woven together with oppressive systems of white supremacy, capitalism and patriarchy, both in its causation and its impacts, means that this crisis doesn't ask us to leave behind what we are already fighting for, but instead to find a way to connect our struggles, our dreams and our liberated futures together so that we are more likely to achieve them all.

For me, as a young Black Jamaican–British woman, growing up in a world where both climate breakdown and violent white supremacy were prevalent in the headlines and experiences of my loved ones, it was this realisation that brought me into this work: the reality that climate action is not only about preventing apocalypse. It's not only about saving my birth island from being fully submerged by rising sea levels. Climate justice – the principle that this book is based on – allows us the real possibility of creating a better world for all of us; a world in which the people who are currently most impacted by the climate crisis are not just saved from climate collapse, but the material conditions for the lives of the most marginalised are also transformed for the better. It offers us a real shot at achieving liberation for every single person, but only if we decide to build it. Now that's something to fight for.

It is absolutely essential for you to understand, whenever you are reading this book, whether it's just after its publication or ten years from now, that it is never 'too late' to take action. It is literally never too late to act to make the world even a little bit better for our fellow humans. Every single fraction of a degree of warming that we can prevent matters. Every. Single. Fraction. Every fraction of a degree prevented will result in a fellow human's life being safer or even saved. That matters. It will never not matter. Please do not give in to doom and despair. Please don't give up.

I won't talk about timelines or when it will be 'too late' to act in this book. The use of timelines or countdown clocks are not as useful as we might think. Yes, when it comes to climate change, timeframes and urgency really do matter. There *are* tipping points, and there are time frames in which some impacts will be made irreversible if adequate action is not taken. But I often feel that the countdown clocks give us the false impression that we can wait eight years, or ten years, or any time other than right now, to take action. It makes us think that we can afford to wait a little longer, when the reality is that these timelines require us to start immediately. They require drastic and urgent action right now. This work cannot wait.

To say that it's never too late to act is not to remove or detract from the urgency of the situation, but instead to say that I believe deep in my soul that there will never come a point at which acting to transform the world for the better isn't worthwhile. I don't want anyone to ever believe that they can't do anything now because they didn't do something before. Whenever you're reading this, whatever has happened, it is never too late to begin to take the actions that will make our world a better place.

Any wins we can achieve really do matter, but ultimately radical change is what's needed, rather than incremental change. The time for slow changes has been and gone. The time for reformism has been and gone. We are now fighting climate-change delayers more than climate-change deniers. Both of them are equally deadly.

For too long, in hoping to 'get everyone on side', the climate crisis has been misrepresented, whitewashed and toned down to be compatible with capitalism; collapsed to only be an issue of science, rather than a rallying cry for the global majority to finally achieve a truly transformed, just world. Too many of the responses to the climate crisis have called for us to simply create a greener version of the same world. We have been told that this is the best we can hope for. Whilst the majority of people care about this huge crisis, far too many have been made to believe that there is nothing meaningful they can do to tackle it.

This is no accident. The fossil-fuel industry is the most powerful lobbying group in the world. They have worked to get their people elected to the highest offices of government. They have prevented fossil fuels from even being mentioned in the biggest international climate agreements, and they have tried their best to turn your attention away from their actions – the real colonial roots of this crisis; the connections it has to other systems of oppression, and the power we have to fundamentally transform this world for the better when we unite against them. This industry – alongside others who benefit from this crisis – wants you to feel small and insignificant. They want you to fall into doom and nihilism. They want you to believe that it's all just too complicated to understand. They want you to believe you don't know enough to do anything. They want you to believe that inequality, oppression and the climate crisis are simply accidental consequences, rather than deliberate choices. They want you to see the change that could create a liberated world as ridiculous, rather than common sense. The elites have toned down your expectations for what *should* be possible in this world, and all because they are truly scared of the collective power that comes when all of us unite to fight for climate justice. To recognise our true power is where transformation begins.

The first half of this book will get you up to speed on who's really responsible for the climate crisis; it will outline what climate justice actually is and focus on who is most affected by the climate crisis, whilst offering an understanding of the oppressive systems that we need to deconstruct. The second half is focused on how we go about tackling this crisis, what to look towards and how to imagine and create the better world we need. This is not a book you simply read, but a book that compels you to act.

Whilst this is a book about the climate crisis, I will not be going into the ins and outs of explaining climate science, or even justifying that climate change is actually happening. To do the latter is to legitimise climate denial as a reasonable and popular outlook, which it quite simply is not. On the former, there are a plethora of resources out there from climate scientists themselves who can explain the science much better than I ever could. Whilst climate science is important, it is not *all* that this crisis is about. Instead, this book is about justice – the part that has been left out of the conversation far too often.

I wrote this book as a Jamaican–British climate activist and student doctor who has been blessed to have learned so much from the wonderful, huge-hearted people I have been surrounded by in the past years of organising for climate justice. I write this book with the deep hope that these words will equip and compel you to join the fight for climate justice. My wish is that this book can be a resource for those who haven't been able to be in those same spaces for various reasons, or for those who have felt shut out or intimidated by the academic nature of climate-justice discourse. This book is a culmination of the ideas that have been running around in my head, but these ideas are not solely my own. Audre Lorde, radical Black feminist and poet, is a huge inspiration of mine, and I come back to her essays often. In one she wrote: 'For there are no new ideas. Only new ways of making them felt.'[1]

The ideas in this book derive from a lineage and ancestry of other humans trying to make sense of the world, liberation, and the climate crisis. This book is my expression of all of this, and everything that I have learned comes from others. I write with the hope that I can make you feel something. I hope that my thoughts and ideas can change things, even if it's in a small way.

Saying that, I hope that this book becomes obsolete. I hope that in the years that pass after its publication, the terminology I use will become dated; the ideas I'm expressing will be antique and that we will have moved far beyond this. I look forward to existing in a time where we have pushed the boundaries for how good, equitable and just this world can be, beyond my current ability to imagine. I am also aware that when writing this book, my perception and understanding of climate justice will be limited by my own position. In this world which promotes ideals of individualism and scarcity, there is a huge pressure to present oneself as infallible or an 'expert'. It would be a disservice to my community and to you the reader for me to posit myself as the definitive voice on this issue, or as someone who knows it all. Whilst the parts of my identity that have meant that I've experienced oppression have informed so much of what I understand about climate justice, I also hold so many privileges that have and continue to protect me from truly understanding the worst impacts of climate change, as I don't experience them directly. I have endeavoured to include perspectives in this book from those who are truly on the front lines of this crisis, and I really encourage you to seek out other voices on this subject beyond mine.

This is the book that I've wished existed for so long. Writing it has transformed me. I believe in my bones that it will do the same for you, and that by acting and coming together we will not only save our world, but transform it for the better.

A NOTE ON LANGUAGE

Language is important. How we choose to communicate and which words we use matter. Language can be used to oppress, but also to liberate. Many oppressive systems are allowed to continue because they remain unnamed. It is for this reason that I often and explicitly refer to 'white supremacy' and 'whiteness' in this book. More on why, and what that looks like, will come a little later, but it's important to say here that I refer to 'whiteness' as a knowledge system. White supremacy is not just people in white hoods or explicit violence; it's a framework of understanding and of knowing the world that was created only a few hundred years ago, along with the construct of 'race', in order to justify the exploitation and harm of some peoples, and the subsequent benefit of others, based on how they are classified under this system. This knowledge system is not a biological reality, but a framework created to divide peoples who have a common enemy: the ruling classes.

I will use the terms 'people of colour', 'Black Indigenous People of Colour (BIPOC)' or 'global majority' to refer to racialised populations who have not been categorised as 'white'. I recognise that these terms are extremely limited, and that they lump together a bunch of very distinct and different experiences, so I have tried to only use them when really necessary to comment on the common experiences of people in these groups. Where possible, I choose to use these terms, rather than others like 'ethnic minority' or 'non-white', as I resist the nature of such terms, which situate the global majority only in comparison to whiteness. Where the term 'ethnic minority' is used, it is only because that was the term used in reports or surveys where the data I reference was from. Outside of these restrictions, I choose to use terminology that comes from communities of colour, rather than ones that have been put upon us by others. We are the global majority, and I think there is a power in remembering that. On that note, when I refer to the working class, that includes a lot of people of colour. Despite what some people may think, working-class people are most definitely not just white.

Often in this book, I discuss disparities in who has caused this crisis and who is impacted. Where possible, I have tried to be specific about the exact countries or areas I am writing about, but there are some instances in which I have had to use more generalised terms, such as 'Global South' and 'Global North', or 'West'. The former emerged as a decolonial attempt to overcome the negative terminology of the 'Third World' to refer to the regions of Oceania, South America, Asia and Africa. The Global North generally refers to countries in Northern Europe, North America, Russia, Australia and New Zealand (Aotearoa) and others. These terms are not used to refer to geography, but rather to global power dynamics and economic inequalities. They are evidently extremely limited and, in my use of them, I am not intending to homogenise the very distinct experiences of these differing nations, peoples and areas.

A few times, I reference 'poor' and 'rich' countries. This is simply because, as with 'ethnic minority', this was the terminology used in the reports the relevant data was from. As I will explain later on, these labels alone can misrepresent how countries come to be seen as poor or rich in the first place. A more useful terminology is to refer to nations in the 'core' and in the 'periphery' of imperialism.

Another term I often refer to in the book is 'material conditions'. By this I mean the environment and living where we cared for each other simply because we all have inherent value as human beings. We were able to see the power that we can all have when we come together, get organised and no longer wait around for someone else to do something. By going beyond solitary, individualised lifestyle changes, I saw the incredible transformation that comes from building community power. By building this power, we can see that settling for just making better choices within a harmful system is not enough; it is only when we come together that we can transform the system itself.

My research into the climate crisis intensified, and I learned about the principle of 'climate justice'. In the mainstream media, the climate crisis has often been coined the 'great equaliser', in that it goes beyond borders and will impact everyone on earth, but the concept of climate justice challenges this notion.

It is true that the climate crisis will affect us all – and that for many of us, that reality is inescapable – but for some, the impact will be, and already is, far greater than for others. Humans in poorer countries are around five times more likely than those in richer countries to be displaced by sudden extreme weather disasters. Within countries such as the UK and the US, those who already experience oppression and marginalisation due to longstanding racial, gender and economic inequalities are disproportionately impacted by climate-related harm through increased vulnerability and exposure to pollution, flooding and other threats.

We might all be facing the same storm, but we are not all in the same boat. Some are in huge, storm-proof, highly polluted ocean liners funded by colonial wealth, whilst others are in small, unseaworthy rafts made more precarious due to the same colonial exploitation which protects others. All people are not equally vulnerable to the climate crisis, and that has a lot to do with historical and existing social and structural inequalities.

The principle of climate justice recognises that the climate crisis is not the so-called great equaliser; in reality, it is the great multiplier. It enhances existing inequalities and oppression and, more than that, it's a product of the same systems that created and inflicted inequality and oppression in the first place; systems that exist to extract and exploit from the global majority for the benefit of a few. But in this recognition also comes the opportunity to tackle the climate crisis in a way that not only stops the bad stuff from getting worse, but actually creates something better. If the climate crisis is based in and dependent on the same systems that inflict violence, oppression and marginalisation of the global majority and nature, then to adequately tackle this crisis requires us to truly *transform* the world for the better of all of us. Climate justice shows us that tackling the climate crisis can also liberate all of us.

It often feels like the goal of modern environmentalism is for the world in its current form – along with its built-in inequality and oppression – to simply *survive*; to carry on, business as usual, preserving the current state of affairs in the world and society. This idea doesn't excite me; it repulses me.

Many come to climate activism with a belief that everything is fine with our current systems, other than the fact that they are causing the climate crisis, as if this crisis is simply an unfortunate accident. The truth is that the climate crisis is the culmination of industries and economies built upon exploitation. Exploitation of the planet and of people is not an unfortunate consequence; it's the very foundation on which the world as we know it has been built.

Grandma tells me that the water is beginning to engulf the land where the colourful restaurants currently sit on stilts. Some of my first memories, which have tethered me to my homeland, feel as if they are being washed away along with the beach. I began to wonder if my descendants will even be able to visit our ancestral lands.

For those of us who are part of the Caribbean diaspora and many other heritage communities, climate change, and its terrifying impact on the lives of our families, is not a question of 'if' but 'when?'

Many of us from these communities have fought against various forms of oppression for as long as we can remember. Even having experienced colonial hardship, some of us have managed to make it through. But of all the injustices, of all the insidious effects of oppression, the climate crisis can feel like an insurmountable feat, and it can leave communities like my grandmother's feeling helpless.

This feeling of helplessness was how I felt about climate change back in 2014. I had just become engaged in climate action and, like so many of us, I was reacting from a place of fear. I had done a little research, and the weight of this huge and impending horror escalated my fear and spurred me into action.

At sixteen, the only activism I understood was that of 'raising awareness' and changing my consumption habits. For many of us, that's all we are told to do. We want to believe that it will be enough. All I knew of the crisis was that it would ultimately lead to our destruction, so I did what many climate-anxious sixteen-year-olds seemed to be doing then: I decided to go vegan, boycott fast fashion and start a blog. I made what I thought at the time were 'radical' lifestyle choices, but I still didn't feel much hope. If anything, the more I focused on these choices and their limited impact, the more acutely aware I became of the enormity of the crisis.

During this period, and against the bewildering backdrop of Brexit and the US election of Donald Trump, like many of us, I would lie awake at night unable to sleep, worrying about the state of the world. This feeling of being completely overwhelmed in the face of these huge crises is not unique – I'm sure it's a feeling you're familiar with too. What makes this all feel so much worse is that we often believe there's nothing we can do; that we have no agency.

Around this same time, I attended one of my first protests: a rally for migrant and refugee rights following the tragic death of three-year-old Alan Kurdi and the media coverage of 'The Jungle' refugee camp in Calais. I moved to the UK from Jamaica at around the same age as Alan died making a similar journey to Europe, though my family made the journey through choice, rather than to flee conflict. The reality of the unjust nature of this world was more obvious to me than ever before. The only difference in my ability to move to this country safely and easily was due to the luck and privilege of having a British father, nothing more. A safe and legal route was not made available to Alan or his family. If it hadn't been for this arbitrary luck, it could have been me on that beach. The world felt like it was hurtling towards an apocalypse and I was angry about it. Getting involved, raising my voice and joining others in demonstration gave me hope.

The hope came from a place of action; we weren't simply resisting the UK government's hostile environment policy or the racist, anti-migrant violence of the French police, we were supporting the building of something impactful; something better. We were helping to create a real community

Truly tackling the climate crisis requires each of us to go to the roots of poverty, of police brutality and legalised injustice. It requires us to move away from capitalist exploitation, which exists only to extract profit. Climate justice offers the real possibility of huge leaps towards our collective liberation because it aims to dismantle the very foundations of these issues. This is a far more exciting prospect to me.

Previously, I had never felt 'seen' in environmental movements, and I didn't feel like they were for people like me. The poster child of climate action was often a white, middle-class hippie, never a Black activist. It seemed as if those taking climate action were doing so because they did not have other, more immediate concerns. In the face of the many manifestations of systemic racism, police brutality and poverty, an 'existential threat' like climate change felt like something that the most marginalised in society would have to deal with later.

Now, I know better. For too long within mainstream media, climate action has been whitewashed, greenwashed and diluted to be made compatible with capitalism. We are living with an economic system which pursues profit above all else; harmful oppressive systems which have heavily contributed to the climate crisis, the environmental consequences of which have been toned down in their presentation to the masses.

Often the aim of this toning-down of the reality of the crisis – and the actions required to tackle it – has been to make the crisis and solutions more palatable. The persisting belief has been that, in order to get the public, industry and policymakers on board with taking action, it can't be too drastic. This has been one of the greatest failures of big green

NGOs and climate campaigners. It's led to a genuine confusion amongst the public in the Global North as to how serious this crisis really is. It's often touted that the actions needed are small, incremental steps to be made on an individual level, rather than what's actually needed: the abolition of fossil fuels and a wholesale transformation of our economic system. This messaging has done the work of Big Oil, Gas and Coal for them. It has allowed for even more climate delay and denial.

For too long, the climate crisis, and ensuing climate action, have been severely misunderstood. Relegated to an existential issue, rather than a present threat to the lived reality of the majority of humans on this earth, the climate crisis has been platformed as an issue for the middle classes, rather than an issue that affects us all, despite the fact that the most vulnerable in society will suffer the most as a consequence of climate change.

In reality, for those of us who are part of diaspora communities, tackling the climate crisis could not be more important. It's our communities in our ancestral homelands who are experiencing the most frequent and worst impacts of this crisis. It's our global communities that are most under threat. Our communities have the most to lose from how this crisis is tackled, but also the most to *gain*. Climate justice asks us not to abandon liberation for our peoples, but to usher it in with even more urgency. The climate-just solutions to this crisis actually offer us a roadmap to a truly better and transformed world.

As a medical student, I found that viewing the climate crisis through the lens of health provided a better understanding of how climate justice can create a better world.

In its 2012 report 'Climate Change and Health', *The*

standards that are accessible and tangible to a person in their life.

Capitalism – our current economic system, which requires and prioritises growth in capital (money) above all else – is discussed frequently throughout the book. If you don't totally understand what capitalism is, or why it's a problem for people and the planet, just hold on until Chapter 4, which tackles it in-depth.

As you'll already have noted, the main intention of this book is to move you into action. By action, I mean engaging in mobilising people and actively building campaigns to fight for climate justice – for example, by organising as a community to campaign against new fossil fuel projects.

I have endeavoured to use the least oppressive language possible in writing this book, but I am aware of my own limitations and I apologise for them. I pray that you are able to hear whatever it is you need to in these pages, and that my own limitations will not get in the way of that.

I've tried to make this book as accessible as possible, but I would also really encourage you to look up any terms you don't already know as you read along. There is no shame in not knowing everything, and so much excitement can come from learning new things. I know that I learned a lot during the writing of this book.

Thank you for deciding to pick it up and read it. I hope with every fibre of my being that you will be transformed – even if only in the smallest way – by it, and that that will transform the world around us. We have a whole, wonderful, transformed world to win. We need you to get there. So, let's get to it . . .

1. WHAT IS CLIMATE JUSTICE?

I've just had a phone call with my grandma in Jamaica, where I've moved for six months. I'm in isolation for the next week or two until I can see her in person, but even being able to FaceTime in the same time zone means I'm closer to her than ever.

I tell Grandma that as soon as her Covid-19 vaccination kicks in and we can see each other in person, we'll visit Hellshire Beach, where I spent so many evenings in childhood. She tells me that this beach, which is only a ten-minute drive from her home, has almost disappeared. I have a sinking feeling in the pit of my stomach. It's a feeling that is not unfamiliar to me. A question lingers at the back of my mind: *How much longer will she be safe?*

The last time I was in Jamaica, in January 2020, I was shocked at how little of the white, sandy beachfront remained.

Lancet described the climate crisis as 'the greatest threat to global health of the 21st Century'. In their later 2015 report, they reframed the threat to 'the greatest opportunity' for global health.[2] Why? Because of the co-benefits that arise when we tackle climate change through the lens of 'justice'.

When we tackle the climate crisis through a justice lens, we are not just making the same world we have now but 'green'. We are choosing to address and transform the oppressive systems that inflict violence on both people and planet. We open up the whole world to transformation, to greater possibilities, to far better than many of us have allowed ourselves to imagine.

We can get an insight into what this can look like by understanding the current situation for many Indigenous Peoples around the world. Many extractive industries drilling for fossil fuels, mining for other minerals or extracting water currently have significant health implications for Indigenous Peoples. My friend Helena Gualinga – who is part of the Kichwa Sarayaku Indigenous community in the Ecuadorian Amazon – spoke out about the reality of children being poisoned by mercury and oil in the water of her community at the closing ceremony of COP27. The health implications felt by Indigenous communities like Helena's are being caused by this poisoning of water, increased noise levels and other multitudinous impacts of the presence of these industries, but those are just the symptoms of a wider sickness. They are just what we see. The reason that this exploitation is allowed in the first place is due to the way that capitalism and white supremacy values both these peoples and nature as a whole. It is these ideologies that allow for and perpetuate this violence and result in these communities being currently under threat, globally. Many

Indigenous environmental human rights defenders (EHRDs) have even been murdered for their activism on the front lines to protect nature and their land. In 2017 – the deadliest year on record for EHRDs – at least 207 murders were recorded across twenty-two countries. Currently, Indigenous Peoples make up only 5 per cent of the world's population but they protect 80 per cent of the world's biodiversity. Recent analysis has shown that unless Indigenous rights are protected, we will fail to keep global temperatures below the crucial 1.5 degrees target set out in the Paris Agreement.[3] By simply existing on their ancestral lands, these communities are forced into fighting the industries attempting extraction there. For many Indigenous Peoples, this fight is not a choice – it's a forced reality.

If we view the health impacts on these communities through a climate-justice lens, then our solutions are not just directed at protecting the health of these communities in the short term, but consider how we can treat the deep cause of the problem rather than just the surface symptoms. In this, the solution of returning sovereignty of land back to Indigenous Peoples is a health and climate-just solution. Indigenous Peoples are the best stewards of their land – they understand how to live in symbiosis with nature. Evidence shows that Indigenous Peoples and local communities with secure land rights vastly outperform both governments and private landholders in preventing deforestation, conserving biodiversity and producing food sustainably. Returning their land to them and protecting that right is a just climate solution which both protects the planet and people. As Max Ajl, author of *A People's Green New Deal*, puts it: 'Land Back is neither surrender nor sacrifice, but the shift which makes the world big enough for all of us.'[4]

The violence faced by these Indigenous communities is not an accident. It's not an unfortunate consequence. Exploitation and violence against marginalised communities and the earth are essential to these extractive industries. It's part of the blueprint. So, to tackle it requires us to go to the root of where it comes from in the first place. To undo the colonial harm of the removal of their land, to return it, is to transform a significant part of the world for the better for us all.

We can also see the correlation between climate justice and the opportunity to improve health in the UK, where inadequate, poorly insulated housing is responsible for a significant amount of emissions, high bills and a negative impact on the health of people in these homes. Insulating homes, installing heat pumps – fully retrofitting homes – would not only significantly reduce energy consumption and therefore help us tackle the climate crisis, but would also make millions of people safer and healthier in their homes and tackle fuel poverty. These homes would be warmer in winter and cooler in summer – tackling the health impacts of extreme temperatures. It would tackle both the cause of health impacts associated with inadequate housing *and* tackle the climate crisis at the same time.

A recent report from the London School of Hygiene and Tropical Medicine detailed how the essential climate action of decarbonising the UK's energy system – that is, moving from fossil fuels to renewable energy sources – would also significantly increase air quality and result in significant improvements in child health. This action could prevent more than 20,000 new cases of asthma and 43,000 premature births. Whilst both of these actions would improve the lives of millions, it is still not a complete solution. We will get into this more in a later chapter.

Climate justice also presents us with the opportunity to transform gender justice and to tackle patriarchal violence. As the climate crisis increases insecurity, conflicts are more likely, famines more commonplace, and women and those from marginalised genders all over the world experience more violence. As the wetlands have dried up in rural Uganda, the communities who farm and live off that land are experiencing food scarcity and instability. In these situations, women have often become a commodity. Some families have even been forced to resort to selling off their daughters for marriage in order to survive.

The climate crisis is making this injustice worse, but if we frame our solutions based on an understanding of this injustice, we can not only stop the exacerbation of this oppression, but actually tackle the root causes of it. Not only because it's the right thing to do, but also because more women in leadership in communities has been found to lead to more climate-compatible actions being prioritised. Therefore, the necessary adaptation measures to droughts in these areas must also include increased access to education for women, domestic-violence protection and other provisions. Framing these actions as climate solutions is absolutely essential.

Many other solutions to the climate crisis also improve racial justice, gender liberation and tackle classism, because these solutions go to the root of the problem, rather than merely treating the symptoms.

As Audre Lorde, visionary writer and Black feminist, said: 'We do not have single issue struggles, because we don't live single issue lives.'[5] Once we see the climate crisis as a justice issue, the solutions will not only prevent climate breakdown, but also make for a better world for all of us.

When we choose to pursue emission-reducing actions which prioritise justice for the most marginalised countries and communities, we combat both the climate crisis and oppression at the same time.

Hilary Graham, a sociologist whose work focuses on the social determinants of health, puts this so clearly: 'Social inequalities become written on the body as health inequalities.'[6] So, when we tackle the crisis with the adverse health impacts at the forefront of our minds, we have the opportunity to make an even better, more equitable world for all of us. We have a very real chance of achieving this better future, but only if we join movements and create this change ourselves.

Climate justice offers us a portal. A gateway from this world into the next. Now, if that's not a rallying call to be part of the movements for climate justice, I'm not sure what is.

It was all of this – the hope, the fear, the excitement, the anger at injustice – that made sixteen-year-old me move beyond 'raising awareness' and changing my lifestyle choices into movements for climate justice and direct action. We *do* have a huge amount of power to radically transform the world, and that power goes beyond individual lifestyle choices and social-media posts. That power comes from campaigning and organising together, in our communities. Today, climate justice is both what I fight for and what keeps me fighting. If it isn't already that for you, I'm certain that our further exploration in the pages to come will make it so.

2. SO WHO'S RESPONSIBLE?

When my grandmother's beloved Hellshire Beach in Jamaica was swallowed up by the sea, it was devastating.

'It's just Mother Nature taking it all out on us. It's happening all over the world and it's just getting worse,' she told me.

I find this sentiment heartbreaking.

The idea that the climate crisis is Mother Nature *punishing* humanity doesn't sit well with me. If it was really about punishing those who caused this crisis, wouldn't it be the billionaires; the richest 1 per cent; the fossil fuel CEOs; the PR firms who have created greenwashing and climate denial who would be experiencing the worst impacts of this crisis? Instead, as we've highlighted, it's those that have contributed the absolute least to creating this crisis who are experiencing the worst impacts. It is a gross injustice.

The idea that a collective humanity is responsible for this crisis is simply false. When just one hundred companies* are responsible for 71 per cent of industrial greenhouse gas emissions since 1988, and the richest 1 per cent of the world produce more than double the emissions of the poorest half of the world, it becomes clear that 'we' did not cause the climate crisis. But it's an idea which has been internalised by so many of us, even my grandma, who has contributed so little to the causation and continuation of this crisis.

It breaks my heart. It also fractures and immobilises our collective ability to tackle this crisis. The idea that the climate crisis is an inevitable fact, that it is the fault of all of us, leads us either into defeatism or into wasting our time blaming each other. Meanwhile, the true big polluters are getting away with it. We need to fight back.

Less than 20 per cent of the world's population is responsible for the consumption of 80 per cent of natural resources. Perhaps unsurprisingly, that 20 per cent is comprised of the richest section of the world's population. It is the model of colonialism being replicated: the South is exploited for the benefit of the rich in the North.

The extent of the warming and the extreme weather patterns we see today are a result of the accumulation of carbon dioxide in our atmosphere over hundreds of years.

---

* Look them up! The Carbon Majors Report details this and more. The culprits are, predictably, mostly fossil-fuel companies, but there are some others in there too. The report also showed that a fifth of global industrial greenhouse-gas emissions are backed by public investment. So something you can do right now to tackle them is to divest your money from them. Find out if your bank still has investments in fossil fuels and if they do, change your bank! It's a quick and easy way you can take action. It won't fix the problem but it's a tactic to get us on the way there.

These cumulative emissions have determined the extent of the climate crisis we now face. As a result, it's incredibly important that we not only look at how many emissions are being produced today, but also who has been emitting the most historically.

Up until 1882, more than half of the world's cumulative emissions came from the UK alone. When we look at excess emissions – the emissions that are causing the climate crisis, as they go beyond the thresholds within which humanity can survive, develop and thrive for generations to come – it gets even worse. A whopping 92 per cent of total global emissions in excess of the planet's capacity have been caused by the richest nation states of the Global North; states like the UK, Canada, the USA and Europe are responsible for 92 per cent of excess emissions. The USA alone is responsible for 40 per cent.

Countries in the Global South, the same countries that are also overexploited for resources and experiencing the worst impacts of climate breakdown, are collectively only responsible for 8 per cent of excess emissions that are driving climate breakdown. This phenomenon is termed 'atmospheric colonialism', in which a small number of high-income countries have historically emitted far more than their fair share. The injustice of this is pretty horrifying.

If you're reading this as someone in a Global North country, thinking *fuck, it's all my fault,* then hold that thought; it's far more complicated than that. It's not simply a Global North versus Global South issue, but rather a case of the actions of a privileged few and the subsequent impact of those actions on the majority of humanity. We'll get into this more later on.

Yes, just by living in countries like the UK, US, Canada and Europe, we do end up with higher 'carbon footprints' than folks in countries in the Global South, but it's also worth considering the fact that the concept of the carbon footprint was first popularised by BP, a company which ranks sixth out of the twenty companies responsible for a third of all carbon emissions since 1965. If one of the biggest fossil-fuel companies in the world is pushing for emissions to be individualised in some way, perhaps it's worth considering who this idea serves?

Guilt can sometimes be a motivator for change – and for those of us living in highly polluting countries, I think some guilt can be helpful, but it can also be a huge distraction. Whilst we are busy blaming our individual lifestyles for this crisis, these bigger companies are getting away with being the true instigators. In blaming ourselves, we are also misunderstanding the ways in which power plays a part in this. In blaming ourselves, or simply focusing on the individual, we are missing out on meaningfully tackling the systems which have caused and continue to perpetuate this crisis.

Whilst some of us do have the power to make changes regarding our individual choices – by taking fewer flights where possible, switching to a renewable energy provider or using public transportation – the reality is that, to even be able to do any of those things, or for it to be viable and accessible for the majority of people to be able to make changes, it's not just up to better individual choices. We will explore this idea in greater depth in a later chapter, but it's important to note that just making so-called 'better' choices – or 'greenwashing' the existing capitalist system – is simply not enough. We have to directly confront the producing class and the system itself.

More than the responsibility of individuals, it should be up to governments to put in place interventions that make these choices more viable, yet many governments are in the pockets of companies who benefit from our destruction. An overhaul of the system is required so that lifestyles that are compatible with sustaining life on this planet are the default, and the bad 'options' that will render Earth uninhabitable have been removed from the equation.

It's also important for us to zoom in even further. Even within these Global North countries, not everyone consumes the same, and therefore not everyone is responsible for the same amount of emissions. More than that, as we have addressed above, when we have been forced into a system that requires and defaults to carbon-intensive 'choices' in order to survive, consumption can't always be equated with responsibility. For example, within Global North countries, many people, and particularly the working classes, are struggling to survive in the face of being exploited by the same companies who are producing climate change.

In 2021, the world was hit with a cost-of-living crisis, perhaps better termed a cost-of-living scandal, given that a small few were making billions when the majority were unable to pay for the things that are essential to live. Energy prices skyrocketed, and in the UK 2.5 million houses with children were plunged into fuel poverty overnight. Households that were already having to choose between heating their homes or feeding themselves were now having to survive on eating one meal a day in a freezing home. Ordinary people were suffering because of an unstable energy system. Behind the scenes, fossil-fuel companies were boasting of multi-billion bumper profits, bragging about not having to pay tax in the UK due to government loopholes, and Conservative government ministers were brazenly accepting thousands of pounds in donations from these same companies. Rather than responding to this crisis by implementing actions that would liberate the UK from being locked into such a volatile and unstable energy system, such as by funding renewable alternatives, retrofitting and insulating homes and funding other infrastructure to decrease energy demand on the grid, the government used the war between Russia and Ukraine as an excuse to push for even more oil and gas, the exact thing which got us into this mess in the first place. Their so-called 'Energy Security Strategy', which provided neither a strategy nor security, did not include a single word on insulation; no windfall tax on oil and gas companies; and nothing on onshore wind. In effect, the strategy did absolutely nothing to help ordinary people who were suffering. What it did do was pump even more government support and resources towards oil and gas. It was even celebrated by the oil and gas industries themselves as a step in the right direction.

To attribute blame or responsibility for consumption or emissions onto the communities who are simply trying to survive under conditions imposed upon them ignores the power dynamics at play. Therefore, it would be false to diffuse responsibility, even within the Global North.

When we talk about responsibility, we must make it clear that a huge amount of responsibility lies with governments, companies and the super-rich, who have consistently acted to ensure that these so-called 'bad choices' were the only ones available. They have created systems whereby millions have been forced into climate-destructive lifestyles simply because these lifestyles generate huge amounts of profit for a small group of people. They have acted to lock so many countries all over the world into fossil-fuel infrastructure for far longer than is necessary. They have enforced and adapted a linear, wasteful economy and forced many of us into it.

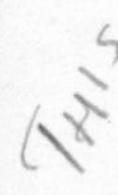

When we talk about responsibility, it must go even further than simply looking at who emits more. It's also about interrogating who it is that has acted to trap us all into these lifestyles. Who is responsible for the fact that we don't live greener lives? Who is responsible for lobbying so hard that governments all over the world are still handing out completely unnecessary and climate-destroying fossil-fuel licences? Who has done all they can to protect their disgusting levels of wealth at the expense of so many human beings' lives?

It's the lobbying groups. It's the capitalist, climate-delaying or -denying right-wing think tanks. It's the fossil-fuel industry. It's every government that has continued to build unnecessary new fossil-fuel infrastructure when they know that we need to choose other options if we want to survive. It's the mining companies. It's the automobile industry. It's the aviation industry. It's the plastics industry. It's every single extractive, polluting body in the world. And even more than them, it's the systems they have come from and uphold: neocolonialism, white supremacy and capitalism. Climate justice asserts that if we want to truly tackle the climate crisis, we must also address the systems from which it originated.

We are in this crisis because of the continual pursuit by Western powers of more and more extraction; more consumption; more economic growth, regardless of the cost. This crisis is the result of many people viewing the value of land and nature as being inextricably linked to its potential for profit. Natural resources have become commodities to be bought and sold.

The vast majority of exploitation and extraction of natural

resources happens in countries in the Global South. From the destructive bauxite mining in Jamaica's Cockpit Country[†] to Shell's oil extraction in the Niger Delta, the mass extraction of fossil fuels and other precious minerals decimates the land, poisons the water and displaces entire communities from their homes. Forests that have existed for thousands of years are destroyed; communities that were able to live off the land are forced into exploitative wage labour in order to survive; and entire ecosystems are eradicated. This all happens so that the majority of these same resources can be taken away to be consumed by people in the Global North to produce profits for a small group. There is a direct transfer of resources – and therefore wealth – from the South to the North.

The colonial reality of the climate crisis – both historically and currently – is finally starting to be recognised, even by the biggest climate institutions like the Intergovernmental Panel on Climate Change, or IPCC, an intergovernmental body made up of thousands of scientists and policymakers who come together to create reports on the most up-to-date and accurate science on where things stand in the climate crisis, as well as predicting what's going to happen in the future. In its most recent report, 'colonialism' was mentioned for the first time. This is historic. Not only was it mentioned, but 'inequity, marginalization, historical and ongoing patterns of inequity such as colonialism' were also named explicitly, with high confidence, as drivers of increased vulnerability for billions of people to climate change.[7] This

† The Maroon communities of Jamaica – descendants of those who led slave revolts and rebellions – have lived in Cockpit Country in the hills of Jamaica for hundreds of years. This area is a protected area, and yet the bauxite mining companies are currently moving ever closer to Maroon lands. Please do look into this issue and help this community to resist.

is something that has been obvious to many people from previously colonised countries for a long time. After decades of work by campaigners, writers and academics, it is finally beginning to be recognised within mainstream climate spaces.

Colonialism created the blueprint for the extractivism that has created, and continues to worsen, this climate crisis. Exploitation, detachment from nature, devaluing of life and violence are all key pillars of colonialism. Colonialism required the dehumanisation of the global majority in order to make the genocidal violence it required to be deemed acceptable. Colonialism created a chasm between humanity and nature. It made us believe that humans are separate from and above nature, rather than part of it, so that the destruction of nature would be justifiable. In the words of Ayisha Siddiqa, Pakistani climate-justice organiser and poet, 'Colonisers go to war with nature and call it a business opportunity.'[8]

Before we continue to explore the links of colonialism and climate, I want to take a moment here to understand colonialism beyond the facts and figures. I want you to pause and remember that behind the huge numbers of those impacted by colonialism were loved humans. Every single person who had their culture ripped from them, who was kidnapped from their own lands, removed from their spirituality, whose families were killed and who had their lives destroyed was a loved, important and immeasurably valuable human, just like those you love in your life. The pain of all of that hurt lives on – and will continue to live on – for as long as there is not justice. Whilst this might seem like a faraway issue from the past, there are many who are still living on and growing the wealth acquired through this violence.

The Runnymede Trust – a UK anti-racist thinktank –

released a report in 2022 in collaboration with Greenpeace, titled 'Confronting Injustice: Racism and the Environmental Emergency', which detailed the colonial history and present of the climate crisis. This report illustrated the legacy of the British Empire in creating the climate crisis.

The barbaric 'slave trade' saw an estimated thirteen million people captured and stolen for profit. Racism was created to justify the mass dehumanisation of kidnapped African peoples, something we will get into in more depth in the next chapter. After this horrendous practice was abolished, the elites of the British Empire searched for a new way to make money. Here began the extractivist fossil-fuel economy.

To fuel the industrial revolution in Britain, the Royal Niger Company colonised large swathes of Nigeria to farm palm oil to grease machinery, and in India ancestral homes were bought and communities displaced so that the land could be exploited to extract dirty coal. Those who had lived off the land were now forced into exploitative wage labour in order to survive as the land was destroyed and the environment poisoned by pollution. A staggering $45 trillion was drained from India to Britain during the tyrannical rule of the empire. The industrialisation and so-called development of Britain relied upon the de-industrialisation of India, in which raw materials were brought back to Britain and exported across the world to create profit held in British hands.[9]

Once the supply for British naval ships was switched from coal to oil, the British government quite literally *bought* the entire country of Nigeria from the Royal Niger Company so that it could give exclusive access to the then-British company Shell to extract from the oil-rich land. Whilst the explicit enslavement and kidnap of Africans was abolished, the violence on these communities did not let up – their lives were still being bought and sold for the profits of the British elite.

In an interview for Runnymede and Greenpeace's report, Lazarus Tamana, President of the Movement for the Survival of the Ogoni People (MOSOP) expressed the persistent colonial nature of Shell's operations, saying: 'Shell's oil operation was built on racism. It operates a double standard, compared to what they are doing in a place like the UK or Europe. Shell completely polluted Ogoniland and the Niger Delta without any sense of guilt. Shell does not care about the local communities in these places.'[10]

Shell continues to operate in the Delta region of Nigeria today, poisoning the rivers so that they can no longer sustain marine life, filling the soil with carcinogens and toxins and destroying the homes and livelihoods of the local communities.

Many of the same fossil-fuel companies still inflicting neo-colonial violence today were also founded during the colonial period, such as British Petroleum (BP), whose original name was quite literally the First Exploitation Company. No joke.

The lies and violence of colonialism persisted beyond the 'British Empire'. Colonialism created a culture of destruction and genocide. This culture is still the basis for how fossil-fuel companies work today.

Fossil-fuel companies are simply neocolonialists. They replicate and perpetuate the colonial model in the modern day. Many of these companies have their head offices and the concentration of their profit and wealth in countries that were the colonisers historically (in the core). They then go from these countries to nations that were previously the colonised (in the periphery) and destroy the land, poison the water and take the desired natural resources back to their home country and retain the wealth that comes from this process. This was made clear in the Runnymede Trust and Greenpeace UK's 'Confronting Injustice: Racism and the Environmental Emergency Report', which detailed how 'six major oil corporations, based in the Global North, account for two-thirds of the world's investment in exploration, profiting hugely at the expense of people living in communities where oil is extracted'.[11]

They are only able to get away with this violence because colonialism normalised and created these actions. We cannot have an honest and meaningful conversation about the damage the fossil-fuel industry has and is causing without talking about colonialism.

Colonialism exploited countries so severely that the impacts are still felt today, in the subsequent climate consequences, the social and economic impacts, and even how we often refer to many previously colonised nations as 'poor' without giving full context as to why that is. As American political scientist Michael Parenti points out, 'Poor countries are not "under-developed", they are over-exploited.'[12]

The exploitation of colonised countries, enacted by countries like the UK, France and other colonial powers, has left billions of people more vulnerable to climate breakdown. The extraction of wealth from these nations and the deliberate underdevelopment of them has left these peoples without the capacity to create the necessary infrastructure to survive the impacts of the climate crisis. Not only have colonial powers inflicted historical violence against so many peoples all over the world in the past, and created and upheld the conditions for extreme global inequity, they have also contributed the most to the creation of a crisis which also hits these same exploited peoples and countries the hardest.

It is because of colonialism that many of the countries most impacted by climate change do not have the ability to be resilient to this crisis. It is because of the wealth inequality generated by colonialism that Western countries are even able to pollute as much as they do. Research by Mary Eleanor Spear and John Tukey revealed that 'most countries that were not colonised during the last five hundred years have a very low mortality rate due to pollution: fewer than 50 deaths per 100,000.‡ That is less than half the mortality rate in countries that have been colonised.'[13]

To be clear, understanding the colonial history and imperial present of the climate crisis is not just a symbolic gesture or 'anti-racist action' to tick off. If we really want to address systemic injustice, oppression and the multiplicity of crises we face, tackling imperialism and white supremacy is essential. It is absolutely fundamental if we want to truly tackle the climate crisis. These ideologies – and ways of organising and distributing power – are the core of what needs to be tackled.

This imbalance of power, this required exploitation, oppression and the creation of sacrifice zones – entire areas deliberately destroyed to allow for production – is what has created the space for a climate crisis to emerge.

We cannot cure this global crisis without addressing its origins. We cannot have climate justice without finally addressing and healing the wounds inflicted by colonialism.

‡ *Reconsidering Reparations* Figure 5.1, refs 44-45

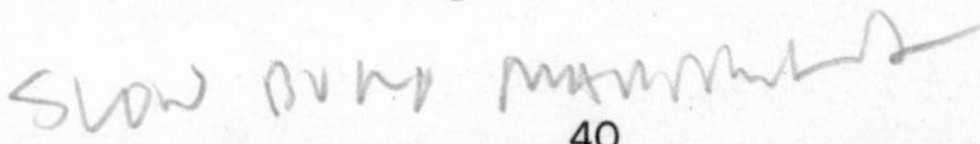

Spending time with my grandma in Jamaica, I learned so much more about myself. My grandma is a woman with a powerful voice, a woman who chooses to laugh whenever she can, a woman who believes that a willingness to act can change the world.

We're sitting in her living-room and speaking more about climate change and its impacts. My cousin jokes that climate change is just a myth, and Grandma grows serious. She is so aware of the threat that this crisis poses for them and she recognises the danger that comes in even joking about it.

The next time we're at Hellshire, we're watching the sea lap up against the restaurants as it now completely covers the place where there once was a beach. Grandma is reminiscing about how we used to picnic and spend time on a beach that is now just water. She asks me what will be done to stop the water. What will be done to protect her and others nearby? So much has already been lost – how can we save what's left?

In these times, the importance of adaptation efforts is highlighted to me; a concept that many can all-too-often be resistant to.

Adaptation actions are things like flood defences, which allow places that are more vulnerable to climate change to have greater protection against its worst impacts. The resistance that many have to adaptation is down to the fact that many see this focus as giving up on preventing the crisis getting worse, because so often that's been the attitude of many Global North nations. The mere concept of adaptation to climate change is only relevant because the North has created a hostile environment, and the responsibility for surviving it has been left with the countries and peoples who have barely contributed to its creation and who have been historically and continually oppressed. The words of Daniel

Ribeiro, a campaigner with JA 4 Change Mozambique, from a panel we did together on climate justice, have stayed with me ever since: 'The West pollutes and the rest of the world just has to adapt.'[14]

It's a pretty grim idea. But adaptation is, sadly, both essential and necessary. There are aspects of climate change that have been made irreversible, and we must take action to reverse whatever we can, but we must also ensure that we protect communities from the impacts they are currently facing. The key thing here, though, is that the responsibility for funding adaptation should be with those countries and companies that have caused the damage in the first place. Nations like Jamaica cannot and should not have to bear the financial burden of adapting to a crisis they did not create. Global North nations must take responsibility here. That needs to go beyond the current empty promises by global governments of 'climate resilience funds'. It has to mean real action.

Adaptation measures must go hand in hand with actions to decrease emissions, referred to as mitigation. We need to stop the crisis from getting worse, make amends for damages already done and protect communities from the impacts of climate change that are yet to occur. It might seem like a tall order, but it's all very doable. Plans already exist that will allow us to do this, so it is essential that we continue to put pressure on our governments whilst also building alternatives outside the existing system.

Alongside adaptation and mitigation, we can't have a conversation about who's responsible for the climate crisis without talking about Loss and Damage. This refers to what has already been lost and/or damaged due to climate breakdown. Whilst adaptation measures are intended to prepare for the coming impacts of climate breakdown, the purpose of Loss and Damage funding is to address the impacts that have already happened. It is often used in reference to the harm that's been caused to nations in the traditional Global South, as that is where most of the existing climate-related breakdown has already occurred.

It's a lot to take on, so let's use an analogy. Imagine the climate crisis as a bath that's overflowing and damaging a home. The tap that needs shutting off is fossil fuels and emissions; the action required to turn off the tap is mitigation. If it were possible to make the sides of the bath higher so that the water couldn't overflow, that would be adaptation, whilst the damage that has already been done to the floor from the water is Loss and Damage. We need to find a way to hold in the water so it doesn't cause any further damage, and we need to address the water damage that's resulted from the overflowing water. We must do both of these things. But, importantly, we need to turn off the tap so that we're not just constantly fighting the mess it's causing.

At COP26, Loss and Damage was high on the agenda for activists, but very low on the agenda for the richest nations who use these conferences as more of a PR conference for them to spout their greenwashing. At COP27, however, after a thirty-year fight, a historic win was made by the most impacted nations and campaigners, as a Loss and Damage agreement was finally made for the first time. Many have referred to this breakthrough as having made the impossible possible, although there is still a lot of work to be done to ensure that the agreement constitutes adequate funds, and that they actually make it to the communities that need them.

Loss and Damage requires the acknowledgement of the fact that climate change is not only happening in the here and now, but has already been causing destruction for decades. Moreover, it requires the acknowledgement that that harm was caused disproportionately by countries in the traditional Global North, and therefore it is their responsibility to pay for the reparation of that harm. Loss and Damage constitutes reparations, and it is essential.

The conversation about the necessity for reparations has been happening for a very long time – it precedes the climate crisis and Loss and Damage. The climate crisis makes the case for reparations more urgent than it has ever been. Reparations are defined by the Oxford English Dictionary as 'The action of making amends for a wrong or harm done by providing payment or other assistance to the wronged party'. Whilst reparations are often represented as being a radical and ridiculous request, they are actually the bare minimum. As discussed earlier, nation states in the Global North – or imperial core – have significant climate debt which must be addressed if all nations are to be able to create the global transition – from climate-wrecking fossil fuels to sustainable renewable energy – required.

Reparations could be what stands between survival or extinction for so many communities facing the worst impacts of climate breakdown. Whether or not reparations should be paid is not a solely philosophical debate – it's a matter of life or death.

The stakes are high for all of us when it comes to the climate crisis. We need global emissions to decrease if we are to move away from tipping points, but currently, for many nations, funding a complete transition away from fossil fuels to renewable energy is simply not financially viable when they are being forced to spend significant funds on repairing the damage of climate breakdown on their infrastructure, paying back debts and living in the persistent oppressive legacy of colonialism. For these transitions to be possible, reparations must be paid to fund them.

In *Reconsidering Reparations*, Olúfémi O. Táíwò makes a renewed case for reparations in the context of climate breakdown. Táíwò frames reparations as a way that we can 'remake the world'. Reparation, he writes, is a construction project:

'But what if the project for reparations was the project for "safer neighborhoods and better schools", for a "less punitive justice system"? That is: what if building the just world was reparations?'[15]

To truly repair the harm that has been done requires more than symbolic gestures or apologies. What is required are concrete actions, investments and transfers of power that will change the persisting conditions that result in the inequality, injustice and increased vulnerability of previously colonised peoples. Reparations must go beyond paying cheques to individuals and instead be investments into infrastructure, education, healthcare, housing and energy. These investments will raise the living standards of all oppressed people, transforming the world as we know it and protecting many peoples from climate change's worst impacts. It's about funding absolutely necessary adaptation and paying to repair the loss and damage that has already happened and a transition to a planet-compatible energy system.

A key component of these reparations includes the cancelling of current debts from previously colonised and currently exploited countries to Global North countries. It is truly astounding that countries like Pakistan, which is one of the countries most impacted by climate breakdown globally, are not only having to try and pay to adapt an entire country to a crisis that its peoples had no hand in creating, but also are having to pay money to the countries who are causing this crisis and damage, as well as being the ones who colonised and deliberately underdeveloped them in the first place.

During the absolutely horrendous flooding that the peoples of Pakistan experienced in August 2022, when one in six people in the country were made homeless in the first few days, many were calling for debt cancellation to be a key part of the response, alongside a move towards reparations. In the same years as this flooding that submerged a third of the country, external debt in Pakistan increased to an astounding 130.2 billion USD in the second quarter of 2022 from 128.920 billion USD in the first quarter of 2022.[16] Not only was Pakistan having to pay to rebuild a third of the country, but also pay back millions and millions in debt to the same countries that caused this crisis. It is truly ridiculous.

For Pakistan, like many other countries in debt crisis,[§] the debt initially arose when the government borrowed money in order to cope with the impact of high oil prices in the 1970s, beginning their high levels of external debt.[17] When the Pakistani government has been unable to pay back these loans, they have had to obtain bailout loans from the

§ Debt Justice assesses countries as being in 'debt crisis' if they have: a large financial imbalance with the rest of the world, either a net international investment position of –30 per cent of GDP or worse, or a current account deficit averaging over 3 per cent per year for three years, as well as large government payments on external debt: government external debt payments are greater than 15 per cent of government revenue. Debt Justice research has found that when external debt payments exceed 15 per cent of government revenue, this tends to lead to a decline in government spending. The IMF says governments tend to struggle to pay external debts once payments are greater than 14–23 per cent of government revenue. You can read more about this on data.debtjustice.org.uk.

International Monetary Fund (IMF).[**] These bailout loans have meant that debt has been passed down through generations, and Pakistan's government has been forced to spend a higher percentage of government revenue on external government debt payments than on healthcare.[††] Rather than restructuring or relieving debt, in the 1980s and 90s the IMF pressured the Pakistani government to increase VAT, increasing taxes for the poorest and most vulnerable in a country where many were already facing extreme poverty. Since then, the debt has only increased as aid has been given in the form of loans and further 'bailouts' by the IMF.

This debt is inherently linked to the climate crisis, imperialism and capitalism. The debt began as a result of fossil-fuels interests and has been exacerbated and continued due to increased costs from multiple disastrous floods. Pakistan's situation is not an outlier – the charity Debt Justice estimates that people in fifty-four countries are currently living in debt crisis, up from thirty-one in 2018 and twenty-two in 2015.

Debt cancellation for the nations most impacted by the climate crisis is the absolute bare minimum that we should all be advocating for. Cancellation of debt will open up these countries to be able to adequately fund an equitable, fair and just transition and adapt to the worst impacts of this crisis. Moreover, as debt repayments have been shown to incentivise extractivism, as they require countries to pursue activities that produce short-term revenue in order to make debt payments, cancellation of debt is also essential for protecting

[**] 'For thirty-two of the last forty-four years, Pakistan has received loans from the IMF, one of the most sustained periods of lending to any country.' – Debt Justice, data.debtjustice.org.uk.

[††] This was true between 1990 and 2016.

nature.[18] It is the responsibility of the countries who have caused and continue to perpetuate this climate crisis to transfer the wealth back into the hands of the peoples who created it in the first place during colonialism and through modern-day work. The exploited should have their resources returned to them so that adaptation and repairing harm and loss can really be possible. Without this wealth transfer, and without debt cancellation, we cannot expect these countries to be able to fund the absolutely necessary transition to renewable energy and infrastructure *and* adapt to climate breakdown.

There cannot be climate justice without materially addressing climate debt.

Rather than being given reparations, far too often the most marginalised communities are used as scapegoats for this crisis. One of the most concerning areas we see is with the dangerous focus on overpopulation as a cause of the climate crisis. Many – mainly white, male – environmentalists or academics have made this argument before. The overpopulation argument states that one of the key causes of climate change is the fact that there are 'too many people'. This simply does not add up when we look at the stats.

Let's use Niger as an example. Niger, a country in Northern Africa, has one of the highest population growth rates in the world, with the population increasing by 3.84 per cent from 2019 to 2020.[19] Due to this, some would suggest that 'controlling' the population in Niger would be a climate solution. However, as a country, Niger also has one of the smallest carbon footprints of any country in the world, ranking 158th for fossil-fuel emissions.[20] Let me put into context how small Niger's climate impact is: in less than one day, the average person in the UK has already created the equivalent emissions of the average person in Niger in a whole year.

That's only one example, but there are many more. Often, the countries with the highest population growth rates are countries made poorer due to historical exploitation. These countries have lower consumption rates per capita (per person) and therefore lower emissions per capita. Research backs this up, finding that nations with the highest population growth rates have had low CO2 emission growth rates.[21] For wealthy nations, the inverse relationship is true. The result is that high-income countries in the Global North have higher per-capita CO2 emissions compared with low-income countries in the Global South. In countries like the UK, with very high per-capita emissions – the UK ranks 17th for fossil-fuel emissions – the populations are declining. The correlation between population growth and carbon emissions is in fact very weak.

But what about China? This is often the first place that springs to mind when talking about population and climate. As the country with the largest population in the world and the country that also tops the emissions rankings, it makes sense. However, when we look at the emissions per capita – how many emissions per person – rather than just for the country as a whole, China goes from first to twelfth. Moreover, it's important to note where the emissions China creates are coming from – what are they for?

China is now the manufacturer of the world. As countries like the UK and the US have decreased domestic manufacturing, much of this has been outsourced to China. Many of the things consumed in these countries are now made in China instead. This means that the emissions required for all of this production are now attributed to

China, rather than the places where these items are actually used. As imported emissions and consumption emissions are not included in national statistics, countries like the UK can boast of reduced emissions and blame the entire crisis on China. The irony.

This is not to say that there is no problem at all with China and climate. However, I think we must interrogate why China is used as a scapegoat for this crisis so often when, historically, it bears much less of the burden. Countries such as the UK and US have been built on a carbon-heavy industrial revolution for hundreds of years, so for them to now turn around and tell others they aren't allowed to do the same feels a bit rich. It's also important to point out that China is accelerating renewables faster than any other country on Earth.

The problem, then, is not too many people. The problem is overconsumption and our wasteful and exploitative system of capitalism. The problem lies with countries in the so-called 'West', not the traditional 'Global South'. What is required is a complete transformation of our society, of the way we consume in the Global North, of our capitalist system. Enhancing women's rights is far more important in tackling the climate crisis than the red herring of population growth.

Now that we've (hopefully) got to the point of realising that the 'overpopulation and population growth is *the* issue responsible for climate change' argument doesn't really hold up, let's ask another important question: why is it so important for us to challenge this argument? Why is it dangerous?

The answer lies in the fact that, when the emphasis is on overpopulation, the solution to this issue becomes, simply, 'fewer people'. If we go back to the origins of the overpopulation argument, we find some pretty horrifying accounts.

In 1968, following a trip to India, population biologist Paul Ehrlich published *The Population Bomb*. In this book, Ehrlich makes the argument that rapid population growth is responsible for resource scarcity, and therefore that population control is a key solution to this. Ehrlich is not alone in this thinking. Others, such as the ecologist Garrett Hardin, took a still more disturbing view:

'How can we help a foreign country to escape overpopulation? Clearly the worst thing we can do is send food . . . Atom bombs would be kinder. For a few moments the misery would be acute, but it would soon come to an end for most of the people, leaving a few survivors to suffer thereafter.'

Arguments like these are entrenched in white supremacy and patriarchy and they compromise the human rights of marginalised individuals. They leave all the culpability for these issues at the door of the most marginalised, whilst failing to address the legacy of colonialism. They damage the perceived value of the lives of people of colour, which has very real implications.

If the problem is 'too many people' then the solution is 'fewer people', right? Often the proposed solutions to overpopulation are family-planning initiatives aimed at particular populations. Whilst, on the surface, this might seem like a positive action, these programmes can compromise reproductive rights instead of enhancing them when they are implemented solely with the intention of reducing a population. The outcomes are especially concerning for those most on the margins; in particular, Indigenous women.

A shocking example of this was seen in the forced sterilisation of Quechua Indigenous women in Peru under President Fujimori's government.[22] Under the guise of population control, 272,028 people were sterilised between 1996 and 2001 under Fujimori's regime. The majority of those sterilised were Indigenous women from poor, rural areas, some without consent.[23] The nature of these programmes is insidious: many of them declare that their intentions are for women's empowerment and environmental protection, but in fact the result of these programmes is the compromising of human rights and the further marginalisation and control of those already oppressed in society. These programmes are almost exclusively targeted at the most marginalised populations and are manipulated by those in power to eradicate populations of people they deem less valuable. When broken down, it simply amounts to eugenics.

Sadly, the Quechua peoples are not the only ones who have been unjustly targeted by these programmes. It was revealed that, as part of population-control projects in Bangladesh, women from lower socio-economic backgrounds were given contraceptives based not on what they actually wanted, but on how difficult it would be for the women to remove them themselves.[24] These projects were conducted under the guise of reproductive liberty and for the climate, but, even if the women experienced the worst side effects from the contraceptives, they were neither able nor permitted to stop them. Anyone who has ever suffered the side effects of birth control can appreciate the horror of this.

It would be wrong to categorically say that there can never be issues with population. Family-planning initiatives can enhance women's rights and liberty, and help to prevent famines, but only if that is the intended outcome of these actions. Problems arise if the intention isn't reproductive liberation and is instead rooted in oppressive and dehumanising ideas.

Ultimately, it seems clear that blaming the climate crisis on overpopulation is false; it dehumanises those who are already marginalised and shifts the blame from those with power onto those exploited by power. The climate solutions we are pursuing must be rooted in justice, otherwise we allow space for violence and oppression. We allow space for eco-fascism.

Eco-fascism can be defined as an ideology that marries white supremacy and environmentalism. It blames overpopulation and immigration for the climate and ecological crisis. Michelle Chan, Vice President of Friends of the Earth, states that the essential thing to understand about eco-fascism is that it is 'more an expression of white supremacy than it is an expression of environmentalism'.[25]

It's an ideology that has been gaining more and more traction in recent years. It has roots in extreme classism and even Nazism.[26] It's been the motivations of Hollywood movie villains like *Kingsman's* internet billionaire Valentine (portrayed by Samuel L. Jackson), who attempts to solve climate change through a worldwide killing spree. Or, notably, Marvel's Thanos, who plans to eradicate half of the living beings in the universe, citing Garret Harding's disgustingly classist 'tragedy of the commons' as his reasoning. But this ideology has also bled into the real world in more and more horrifying ways.

Overpopulation, a hatred of immigrants, and eco-fascist ideology were all stated as motivations by the shooters in two separate mass killings in 2019:[27] first, the El Paso shooting, an act of domestic terrorism and the deadliest attack on Latinos in modern American history; and second, the Christchurch shooting in New Zealand, which targeted Muslims and killed fifty-one people. More recently, the Buffalo shooter – who murdered ten people in a majority-Black neighbourhood in New York – also attributed his motivations to eco-facism. Eco-fascism is deadly for already marginalised communities.

But these ideas are not just promoted by conventional villains; they're also promoted by far too many old, white, legacy environmentalists and conservationists who consistently cite 'overpopulation' as the main cause of climate breakdown.

Many who use the overpopulation argument do so because it is convenient for them. These people don't criticise the systems from which they benefit: Western capitalism, overconsumption and wealth inequality. Instead, the issue is presented as distant.

We cannot allow space for even more violence against marginalised people to be disguised as 'climate action'. We must challenge it wherever we see it and keep values of justice and equity close to us. Whilst climate justice offers us a roadmap to a better world, eco-fascism could create an even worse one.

Whew. That's a lot. I know it is. I said this was a book about hope and I was being honest about that, but for us to get there, we first have to understand where we are at now. Once we understand where we are, we can work out how to navigate away.

So, who *is* responsible? It's not women of colour in the Global South for having a family; it's not just China; it's not those on the front lines of climate breakdown. It's the fossil-fuel companies that have created this mess, funded climate denial and murdered activists on the front lines. It's every government that has acted in the interests of these multi-billion dollar companies, rather than for the people. It's the super-rich; the billionaires; the one hundred companies. It's overconsumption, capitalism and white supremacy.

Whilst *we* might not have caused this crisis, we have to be the ones to tackle it. We all have a responsibility to our fellow human beings to try and completely transform this world for the better. We all have a responsibility to protest, to fight back, to campaign, to talk to our friends and family about this and to respond to calls of solidarity from our oppressed siblings all over the world. We all have a responsibility to take this into our own hands and change the world, because change is not passive. Things don't – and won't – just get better over time. We have to take action in order to make things better. We have to join movements and take drastic action because the world as we know it quite literally depends on us doing so.

The reality is that absolutely everything about this world will have to change. What brings me hope is that, as economist and writer Naomi Klein puts it, 'the nature of that change is up to us'.[28] If we continue with business as usual, the result isn't that the world as we know it will simply continue; predictions of climate modelling by scientists have shown that the destruction caused by warming would leave us with a markedly different Earth. The other option is to drastically change everything we know to tackle this crisis; to tackle injustice and transform the world to a system that works for and protects both the people and the planet.

I know which change I would prefer. I also know that it won't happen passively. Change is an active process. There are no superheroes coming to save us; there is only you and me, and all of us together. If we want the world to be transformed; if we want a liveable future; if we want a world where we are all respected and safe, then we must all take action, now. We all must realise that we all have a responsibility to act, and a role in the action that's perfect for each and every one of us. We must all join movements and work together to resist oppression.

3. BEYOND WHITE ENVIRONMENTALISM

There often seems to be a sort of bemusement around why it's taken so long – and why there is still so much delay – around tackling the climate crisis. There are, of course, many reasons for this. As we discussed in the previous chapter, there are the lobbying groups in the fossil-fuel industry who have invested billions in climate-denial campaigns, promotion of false solutions and other delaying tactics. There is our economic system of capitalism, which has prioritised profit over all else. But it is also impossible to ignore the fact that some of the original climate science conducted in the 1970s – and then buried – by the fossil-fuel giant Exxon revealed where the worst impacts of the climate crisis they were causing would likely be felt.

As a result of this research, both Exxon and, shortly afterwards, governments globally, knew that the climate crisis would most likely hit Global South nations first and hardest. They knew that this would devastate entire communities, but they decided not to act to save them. In fact, they continued to make this crisis even worse. It was decided that profit was more important than human lives.

Specifically, they decided that profit was more important than the lives of these particular people, globally. These particular people were mostly people of colour. That was a choice. The fact that climate action has only begun to speed up now that Global North, majority-white countries are coming under threat is also a choice. These choices come from the myth that some lives are more valuable than others. This myth is white supremacy.

Would we have seen as much delay and denial if the countries most impacted by this crisis were majority-white countries in Europe or North America?

Whilst so many have said that the climate crisis is the 'first existential threat', essayist Mary Annaise Heglar challenges this notion. In her essay 'Climate Change Isn't the First Existential Threat', she details how for Black and Indigenous communities, particularly in the Southern United States, existential threats are nothing new:

'For 400 years and counting, the United States itself has been an existential threat to Black people. Let's be clear: slavery didn't end with freedom; it just morphed into a marginally more sophisticated, still deadly machine.'[29]

Whilst these existential threats are not new, they are being amplified by this crisis. The refusal to act – and in fact to make it worse – is white supremacy in action. It is genocidal. It would be a disservice to call it anything other than that.

In the last chapter, we discussed IPCC reports, which comprise a compilation of all the climate science in the world. As well as being the first time that colonialism was mentioned in any of their reports, their most recent report was also billed as 'Code Red For Humanity' in the media.

One key thing to note about the IPCC's reports is the fact that governments sign off on them. Specifically, they sign off on the briefing for policymakers; that is, a shorter, more accessible summary of the report. The reason I'm putting so much emphasis on this here is because, for years, governments have been signing off on extremely detailed reports that make it incredibly and increasingly more clear that Western countries are willingly sacrificing so many other communities. Each report gets more and more accurate about where exactly these impacts are happening. Governments have signed off on reports that have detailed exactly how and when island nations like Kiribati and Tuvalu in the South Pacific will be submerged by water. They've signed off on reports that have detailed what actions can be taken in order to prevent this. Rather than taking these necessary actions, they've done the opposite. The delaying, denial and so-called 'inaction' we are seeing by governments on climate change is a willingness to sacrifice the Global South, just so that capitalism can continue and a small percentage of extremely rich people can continue to be extremely rich. It is ridiculous to see climate inaction as anything other than white supremacy at large. This so-called 'inaction' isn't passive – it is violence.

It also feels inaccurate to refer to this complete refusal to take the proposed actions as 'inaction' when governments are still actively giving out fossil-fuel licences. It's not really 'inaction' when the very companies causing the crisis are given billions in public money as subsidies. Nor can the creation of policies that work in the interests of the fossil-fuel industry, rather than the people, truly be thought of as 'inaction'. Heglar shares this frustration:

'Nothing about [the government's actions] is passive. The climate crisis is the result of government collusion, not government inaction.'[30]

The devastating flooding in Germany in July 2021, which killed 184 people, made the climate crisis hit home for so many who had previously thought they'd be safe from it. It should not have taken white people experiencing climate breakdown in order for this crisis to be taken seriously when flooding in India and Bangladesh in the previous year killed over a thousand people. There should not have been as much disbelief that this sort of devastation could happen in Europe. Much of this disbelief comes from the idea that whiteness and Western privileges will always protect you. As the climate crisis gets worse, all of us must realise that there will come a point where privileges cannot keep you completely safe. It's therefore important to form a connection to this crisis in a personal way because the climate crisis is coming for all of us.

The whiteness I am referring to is not just about the colour of someone's skin. 'Whiteness' is a social construct. The idea of race was created in the 1800s in order to justify the enslavement of kidnapped African people and to prevent strong coalitions being built between Black enslaved people and white workers. The ruling class created this system in order to uphold and maintain the unequal distribution of power which benefited them. 'Race', and by extension 'whiteness', was created to maintain power in the hands of a few.

It is absolutely vital to recognise that the construct of race and whiteness was created in order to justify the enslavement and violence inflicted on human beings kidnapped from Africa. It has never been simply about prejudice or not liking the colour of another person's skin. From its inception, and still today, whiteness and white supremacy are mainly about power.

To understand this fully, and to recognise how the system of white supremacy is still operating today, we need to understand how the world currently works. We need to understand imperialism.

Under our current economic system of capitalism, which we will explore in more detail in the next chapter, inequality is a necessity. Since the first colonists arrived on the shores of the Americas, Africa and Asia, the power of nations in the core of the empires has been used to oppress the nations on the periphery. In order to fund lavish lives for some and produce high yields of cheap goods, exploitation and extraction from colonised countries was made a necessity. This continued past the 'age of colonialism' and persists today.

In *A People's Green New Deal*, Max Ajl writes:

'Wealth and well-being concentrate in the nations called cores, and poverty in places called peripheries and semi-peripheries. It is a feature, and not a bug, of capitalism that wealth piles up amongst the few and poverty piles up amongst the many.'

This power that is exerted by nations in the core on nations at the periphery is called imperialism.

As Ajl continues:

'The capacity to produce wealth is not because core countries are exceptional other than in their use of violence against the periphery. These concepts allow us to think of the wealth of the core as based on the poverty of the periphery.'[31]

Due to world trade rules, continued economic dominance by the Global North is maintained, with the economies of the North still being reliant on cheap labour and extraction of 'natural resources' from the Global South. For the continuation of this structure of extreme inequality and overconsumption, which is incompatible with life on this earth, there need to be areas and peoples that those with power in the North are willing to sacrifice. Imperialism necessitates sacrifice zones.

Sacrifice zones can be defined as communities located near the most intensely polluting and dangerous facilities, including open-pit mines, smelters, petroleum refineries, chemical plants, coal-fired power stations, oil and gas fields, steel plants, garbage dumps and hazardous waste incinerators.[32] Sadly, there are already thousands of examples of sacrifice zones all over the world. These zones are concentrated in communities that are already made vulnerable due to systems of oppression and are disproportionately in the Global South.

Research from a report on sacrifice zones by the UN Special Rapporteur on Human Rights and the Environment details some of the horrendous impacts. As a result of extractivist oil companies like Shell, the people of the Niger Delta have and continue to experience significant physical and mental-health problems. Perpetual gas flaring and oil pollution have resulted in abnormalities in blood, liver, kidney, respiratory and brain functions. Further to this, asthma attacks, headaches, diarrhoea, dizziness, abdominal pain and back pain have also all been reported as adverse health effects. As a result, the average life expectancy for the residents of the Niger Delta is only forty years of age. Forty years. That's fifteen years less than the average life expectancy of Nigeria as a whole.

Another sacrifice zone can be found in Northern Colombia, where a massive open-pit coal mine – El Cerrejon – has created vast amounts of air pollution in excess of WHO guidelines, contaminated the local water supply, produced significant noise pollution and put workers under elevated risks. Residents in the surrounding areas have been found to have high rates of respiratory illness and have elevated levels of toxic substances in their blood. The neighbouring Wayuu Indigenous communities live in extreme poverty, with half of Wayuu children suffering from malnutrition and stunted growth. Meanwhile, the transnational mining companies that run El Cerrejon have generated billions of dollars from the mine.

In occupied Palestine, water is syphoned off from the West Bank by the Israeli state, who continue to restrict water access for Palestinians. The theft of natural resources from the Palestinian people, combined with the persistent violence and invasions, makes Palestine an increasingly more hostile place to exist. The situation is one of climate apartheid, and it's no accident.

These sacrifice zones haven't occurred by accident; rather, it's another example of the colonial model being replicated. The level of 'sacrifice' required in order to maintain these dynamics of power and economics will get bigger and bigger as the climate crisis intensifies, unless we do something to radically change the current model our world operates on and truly liberate oppressed peoples.

Whilst the most stark examples of these sacrifice zones are in areas in the Global South, the same patterns of placing hazardous operations next to communities of colour also happens in the Global North. This phenomenon – in which communities of colour are disproportionately exposed to pollution and hazards – is called environmental racism.

In the UK, this manifests with people of colour, those living in areas of high deprivation, marginalised groups such as refugees and asylum seekers, disabled people and those experiencing homelessness, all being made more vulnerable to the negative health impacts of climate change.[33] Evidence has shown that people of colour are more likely to live in areas most impacted by environmental disadvantage, concentrated in low-paid jobs and more likely to be living in fuel poverty.

Whilst growing up in a majority-white area led me to personally experience more interpersonal racism, it also protected me from experiencing systemic and environmental racism. Areas of the UK that are populated by majority communities of colour are more likely to be situated next to incinerators – with almost half of all existing incinerators situated in areas with high populations of people of colour.[34] One of these incinerators is located in Edmonton, in the same area where some of my Jamaican family lives; descendants of my grandma's brother, who moved to the UK in the 1970s.

Sixty-five per cent of the residents in Edmonton, a town in North London that is one of the most deprived areas of the UK, are people of colour. It's also home to the largest incinerator in the UK: the Edmonton EcoPark waste incinerator. Despite protests from local residents and groups over the significant health risks that this incinerator poses for the community, the incinerator is still operational and was even approved for renovation in 2017.

It's not just Edmonton residents who are forced to breathe in extremely polluted air. The London Borough of Newham has both the highest Black, Asian and ethnic minority population and highest level of air pollution in England. Lambeth, which has a higher than average Black population, also has nitrogen-dioxide levels in the air that are almost double the guidelines of the World Health Organization's recommendations. Studies have shown that Black people in London are more likely to breathe illegal levels of air pollution than white and Asian groups. In the report 'Confronting Injustice: Racism and the Environmental Emergency', activist and academic Alexandra Wanjiku Kelbert of Black Lives Matter UK (BLMUK) describes these 'sacrifice areas':

'From Blackpool to Newham, the most deprived areas and communities are sacrificed to make room for roads, for airports, for polluting industries, and for profit. Statistically, it's no surprise that the first person in the UK to potentially have air pollution listed as a cause of death is a Black girl from Lewisham; nine-year-old Ella Kissi-Debrah suffered a fatal asthma attack in 2013 after pollution on the road near her house repeatedly broke legal limits in the years leading up to her death. Campaigns like Clean Air for Southall and Hayes (CASH) are yet another painful reminder that the most toxic substances, most dangerous industries and the most polluted roads are in the backyards of the poor, which in this country all too-often means the backyards of Black people and people of colour.'[35]

In 2020, as George Floyd was murdered by a white police officer suffocating him with his knee on his throat, his last words, 'I can't breathe', became a rallying cry against racism all over the world. What hit home for so many Black communities globally was how not only could they metaphorically not breathe because of the oppressive manifestations and confines of white supremacy, but also that so many Black communities *literally* cannot breathe because of environmental racism. Similarly to Black communities in the UK, Black Americans are also more likely to live near landfills, industrial plants and fossil-fuel infrastructure. The process by which this hazardous infrastructure is deliberately situated close to African American communities is called redlining. This process means that fossil-fuelled power plants, refineries and hazardous-waste facilities are disproportionately and deliberately situated in Black or ethnic-minority neighbourhoods. As a result of this, Black Americans are three times more likely to die from exposure to air pollutants than their white counterparts.[36]

Given these realities, it is completely ridiculous to separate climate justice from racial justice or class justice. The climate crisis and white supremacy are inherently linked in more ways than one. We simply cannot talk about the climate crisis without interrogating white supremacy. These issues are absolutely inextricable from each other. Without acknowledgement of this, without inclusion of racial justice into our climate action, our climate actions are incomplete. Without inclusion of racial justice, our actions risk upholding oppression and allowing the systems that rely on violence to adapt and exist for longer.

The sickness that is white supremacy is killing us all, some more quickly than others.

It has made our world sick through creating colonialism, which provided the blueprint for the fossil-fuel industry's land grabs and violent extraction for fuel that led to the climate crisis. It's made our movements sick by excluding and silencing the voices of those most impacted by this crisis. White supremacy has both created this problem and held us back from solving it, even in the spaces that say they're there to create change.

This myth of white supremacy – and indeed, the myth that is whiteness – is all that many of us know. It has invaded and seeped into all of our spaces. This ideology has quite literally colonised the entire world, both physically and mentally. It has built economic systems, borders, nations and even formed how we think about ourselves and each other. It has propagated the belief that we are in hierarchies – that we are separate from nature and one another. No wonder it has permeated the environmental movement. Whiteness, like race, is a social construct – a story that we are told. A story of domination, of superiority, of hierarchy, pursuit of perpetual growth at any cost and perpetual crisis. Let's tell another one.

But as this is simply a harmful myth, what else could we believe in instead? Where else could we be putting our attention? What is beyond white environmentalism? For us to find that out, let's first interrogate what white environmentalism actually is.

I've found reading a lot of books about climate hard. Strangely, I didn't realise why this was for a long time. I was deeply interested in both understanding the climate crisis itself and how to tackle it. I also loved books and reading. But for a long time, every time I picked up a recommended read on climate, it just felt a bit . . . icky. I didn't feel like I was being pulled into their vision of how the world could be, or even the way they saw it now.

So many of these climate books are written by white men. The perspective was often about the 'discovery' of nature and the accounts of nature from colonisers. Often the solutions proposed seemed to be ones that would either restore the world to how it was when these colonisers first arrived on the world's continents, or simply to allow the world as it is now to continue without the looming threat of climate change. They didn't go much deeper than that.[‡‡]

A lot of my first experiences in the climate movement were very similar. I would be told time and time again that I

---

‡‡ I also have to note here that I've read many books on climate in more recent years that have gone beyond white environmentalism and profoundly impacted me. Many of those books I mention in this book and I am so grateful for each of the authors for writing them.

shouldn't dilute the message by talking about racial justice as well as the climate. I would be told that racial justice was too distracting or complicated and that we should 'just focus on the science'. Often, in attempts to explain why racial justice is inherently linked to the climate crisis, the response from some white people in the movement was that we needed to 'focus on the most important issue: climate change'. The very real worries of Black, Indigenous and people of colour (BIPOC) and our experiences of racism in this world were minimised. We were told that the climate crisis was bigger than these issues and therefore that it should be addressed first. Our oppression was said to simply be getting in the way of progress on climate action. There was a subtext beneath it all that we didn't really matter to the movement unless we were being useful to it for their vision. In these spaces, our vision was rarely included.

What is so deeply frustrating about this idea of focusing on one single issue at a time is that it holds all of us back. Having a climate movement that addresses oppressive systems of white supremacy, classism and capitalism not only benefits the majority of people but could also inspire the majority into collective action. The same systems that are causing harm to individuals and communities racialised as Black also cause harm to others in society. Capitalism, white supremacy and imperialism are all inherently connected. We will explore this more in the next chapter.

Far too much of my time in the climate movement has been spent fighting other people's messes or having to explain over and over again why we need to care about tackling racism and white supremacy as part of our climate work. It's absolutely exhausting and has led me to burnout many times.

Too many white-majority climate groups have glorified arrest, putting their Black members at increased risk of violence from institutionally racist police. As Black people are three times more likely to be killed by the police in the UK than their white counterparts and are already disproportionately incarcerated and policed, risking arrest is not the same for everyone. In many of these spaces, the humanity and value of Black lives is disregarded.

After far too many years pushing from inside these groups, I've begun to realise the importance of creating spaces for BIPOC activists – and in particular for Black activists – to be able to exist and organise without all this added stress. Spaces where we don't have to code switch – that is, express ourselves differently from our authentic selves in order to stay safe or fit into a white space – or be 'less'; where we aren't expected to represent an entire community, or fight with comrades. Spaces where we do not have to constantly push for the fullness of our humanity to be acknowledged.

Partway through writing this book, I went to New York City with The Bad Activist team to work on strategy for the group, who are based all around the world. This trip solidified my resolve to prioritise BIPOC climate spaces. Spending a week with almost exclusively BIPOC climate folks was a completely unparalleled joy. It refilled my cup.

Many months later, when Leah Thomas, author of *The Intersectional Environmentalist*, reached out to pull together a bunch of incredible Black climate-justice activists[§§] to

---

[§§] Shoutout to Dee, aka The Black Feminist Bookshop, Wanjiku 'Wawa' Gatheru, Arielle V. King, Sheena Anderson, Marion Atieno Osieyo, Tatu Hey, Daze Aghaji, Calah Singleton, Joycelyn Longdon, Einass Bakhiet and Beau Boka Betesa for being the incredible Black Ecofeminists who organised and spoke that day.

organise the first Black Ecofeminist Summit in the UK as part of her UK book tour, I absolutely jumped at the opportunity to work together to create a bigger version of the joy and acceptance we felt in NYC for other Black environmentalists. The day was one of the most beautiful experiences I've had, taking part in the programming for the event and joining in conversations about how we can build, find joy and resist in ways that do more than just centre our trauma.

After that day, I was speaking to my friend and fellow British–Jamaican Dominique Palmer, who had been there with me, about how healing it had been. Both of us have experienced huge amounts of racism from within the movement and it has made us both want to quit so many times. We expressed to each other how this was the first time that we had felt like we could be fully ourselves in movement spaces. That freedom allowed us to find joy within the work. It allowed us to laugh. It made dreaming of the new world we are working towards so much easier. Our dreams and our imaginations are so powerful in this work. To share time with Black climate activists focused on joy rather than just trauma is so precious. We need more spaces that allow for that.

But how do we reconcile this need with the need for building coalitions between communities? It is true that we will need to work with and form alliances with people who don't totally agree with us on everything, but in order for this work to be sustainable in the long term for those of us who experience interpersonal racism because of how we are racialised, we also *need* to have spaces where we are safe and cared for too. We need those spaces in order to continue. Otherwise, we burn out.

As someone who has experienced significant racial trauma, I've come to realise that this is essential for me. It doesn't make me a worse activist or mean that I care less about coalition building; it just means I actually care for my well-being and my longevity in this fight. It also allows me to remember what I am fighting for and that I'm not alone. We can and must find the balance of having those safer, more regenerative organising spaces for those of us with racial or other forms of trauma, whilst not becoming isolationist and separatist in our work.

I've realised that if I want to continue with this work for the rest of my life, I need to take care of myself. I need to find and prioritise joy. I need to be able to be my full self: a soft Black girl. I need to be living a life that feels like it's worth fighting for.

So, I can't keep exclusively putting myself into spaces where my authentic self isn't valued or welcome if I can avoid it. I can't have my sense of self continually ground down, especially if there is another choice – and there is often another choice. There are groups that are for and by BIPOC communities, and even more of them are springing up every day. These groups are also working on a collective vision for all of our liberation. We can create safer spaces for ourselves and we must if we want to keep going.

The long-term goal is that our organising spaces are actually safe, and that's when accomplices can come in. If you're someone racialised as white reading this, you've got to do the work to make the mainstream environmental movement safer and anti-racist. Dr Ayana Elizabeth Johnson, marine researcher and climate communicator, puts the case for the necessity for anti-racism work for climate action so well in her op-ed, 'I'm a Black climate expert. Racism derails our efforts to save the planet', for the *Washington Post* during the Black Lives Matter uprisings of June 2020:***

'So, to white people who care about maintaining a habitable planet, I need you to become actively anti-racist. I need you to understand that our racial inequality crisis is intertwined with our climate crisis. If we don't work on both, we will succeed at neither. I need you to step up. Please. Because I am exhausted.'[37]

Hard same.

When I refer to 'white' environmentalism, I refer to environmentalism that is based on maintaining the existing status quo; environmentalism that strives for preservation of how things are now rather than transformation of the world as we know it. As much of mainstream 'environmentalism' in the West emerged from white men wanting to preserve nature for their enjoyment, it has completely ignored any calls for real justice or transformation. The focus was on 'conservation' and leaving nature untouched and pristine. In fact, this form of environmentalism, which sees humans as separate from nature, actually compromises human rights. In the pursuit of 'conservation', Indigenous communities like the Maasai in Tanzania – who are part of nature and are the best stewards of the land they have lived on for generations – have been evicted from their lands and experienced violence.

White environmentalism is environmentalism that is Euro- or Western-centric in its vision for climate action. Environmentalism that has tunnel-vision on emissions, and leaves out ideals of justice. Environmentalism that proposes 'solutions' that can actually have unjust consequences.

*** Go read the whole article. I think about it often!

White environmentalism says that, in order to solve the climate crisis, we just need to buy carbon offsets, electric vehicles, plunge investment into carbon capture and storage and all go zero waste overnight. It doesn't call for any real material changes in the systems that have caused climate change, but instead calls for 'solutions' that allow for adaptations of these harmful systems. It calls for ways for these systems to continue to exist.

These solutions are often false, not just because they don't go to the root or the core of what's caused this crisis, but because many of them are simply inefficient for what we really need. Moreover, they actually damage ecosystems, biodiversity and compromise human rights. They are false solutions because they don't solve the problem. They just stick a Band-Aid on it. They are a way to distract from and delay the solutions we really need. They take attention away from the real solutions: abolishing fossil fuels, abolishing extractivism and dismantling capitalism. Instead, they simply attempt to greenwash capitalism.

Let's take electric vehicles (EVs) as an example here. Often, a climate solution suggested – mostly by car companies themselves – is to simply replace every diesel and petrol car with an electric one. If this were to happen, the argument goes, it would significantly reduce emissions. That's a good thing, right?

The problem with this being presented as a solution is that it refuses to acknowledge the exploitation of both people and the land that is inherent in the manufacture of electric vehicles. One of the natural resources required for these EVs is lithium. Lithium is the lightest metal on earth and is used in batteries to power electrical and electronic goods. The push for more EVs has led to a significant increase in the demand for lithium. Due to poor recycling systems, the vast majority of this lithium is extracted from the land, with the majority of this extraction happening in Bolivia, Chile and other Andean nations. A report by Friends of the Earth Europe found that this extraction pollutes and depletes the surrounding waters, and toxic chemicals involved in the extraction process have caused horrendous harm to communities, ecosystems and food production.[38] These impacts have led to water-related conflicts between communities in Northern Chile and contamination of the main water sources for the people of Argentina's Salar de Hombre Muerto.

Presenting EVs as a solution tunnel-visions on specific emissions – those involved with driving the vehicle – and ignores the other climate and human impacts involved. It completely ignores the fact that a significant amount of the emissions from vehicles actually come from the shipping of resources used to make them all over the world as they are manufactured. To produce enough electric vehicles to replace every existing vehicle would create a truly momentous amount of emissions. Moreover, it just looks at the world exactly as it is now and tries to make a 'green' replication of it – something that is referred to as greenwashing or green capitalism. We can do so much better than this.

Rather than expecting every single person who requires transportation to be able to buy a fully new EV and create so much more environmental damage and exploitation through production, why not reduce the number of vehicles on the road in the first place by creating better and cheaper public transport? Why not invest the money that would be going into EVs into trains, electric buses and lithium recycling systems to use what we have already extracted and create more infrastructure to enable cycling and walking to become more viable forms of transport? Transportation like this would not only significantly reduce emissions, but it would also require less production, less exploitation of minerals from the land, create fewer polluted and congested cities and provide cheaper transportation for all. Solutions like this would have a far greater impact on reducing emissions and tackle a multitude of problems that are currently caused by the individualised transportation system.

It's also important to open up the conversation around carbon offsets. In the past, I've believed in their role and importance, which I think came from me wanting to believe that it could be that easy. Climate offsets are basically a form of credit that you can buy to balance out an amount of emissions. Whether it be for a flight or for your entire carbon footprint, offsets sell you an idea that you can buy off those emissions for only a few pounds. When you buy an offset, you're often told you're buying trees or supporting other climate-positive projects that will 'offset' or balance the CO2 produced from your actions. This is not to say that all of these offsets are false; removing carbon from the atmosphere where possible is important, but we need to really interrogate these projects.

It's been revealed that many of these so-called climate-positive projects have actually displaced Indigenous peoples from their lands, inflicted violence against them, or resulted in more damage to the existing biodiversity by replacing the existing ecosystem and planting monoculture. The majority of these projects are often placed in traditional Global South countries, whilst the offsetting companies are owned by Global North countries. These offsetting projects have then perpetuated the same model of land-grabbing and human-rights abuses from colonialism, with these Western companies buying off huge swathes of land to balance out the climate guilt of Westerners. This process has been termed by many activists as 'CO$_2$lonialism'.

Many governments around the world are complicit in CO$_2$lonialism. Since 2014, the Sengwer Indigenous community in Kenya have been violently driven off their land in order for it to be used to plant trees to offset EU emissions.[39] This land is the place where this community has lived for generations – it's land that this community understands how to look after better than anyone else. But the Kenyan government is evicting them to satisfy this deal so that they can use it to so-called offset emissions. It's absolutely abhorrent.

In occupied Palestine, tree-planting projects to offset Israel's emissions have displaced Palestinians from their homes.[40] There, offsetting has been used to greenwash what is fundamentally settler colonialism. It is not justice.

The idea of 'Net Zero' is also a false climate solution. Whilst the goals put out by governments and corporations that they will reach a 'net' zero of emissions by a certain date might seem promising, in actual fact these targets just allow for responsibility to be evaded and climate action to be delayed. The *NOT-ZERO* report,[41] conducted by a coalition of organisations, details these problems. The thing is, 'Net Zero' is not actually 'zero emissions'.

In principle, 'Net Zero' plans require governments and corporations to detail how they will balance out the emissions they produce with 'climate-positive' projects. The aim is that through this balancing, the damage caused by these emissions can be levelled out.

In practice, this allows for a loophole for governments and corporations. Net Zero does not encourage an actual decrease in emissions. Instead, it allows you to pay your way out of the emissions produced. The 'climate-positive' projects that are invested in to balance out emissions are offsets and Bioenergy with Carbon Capture and Storage (BECCS) tree plantations. We've already explored why these can cause problems and compromise justice, but there is also quite simply not enough available land on the planet to accommodate all of the combined corporate and government 'net zero' plans. A landmark study by over twenty scientists – *The Land Gap Report* – revealed that 1.2 billion hectares of land would be required to be used for carbon-removal projects to fulfil global governments' climate pledges. That's the same amount of land that is currently used for all crop lands globally. It's completely unrealistic that this much land could sustainably, ethically or even reasonably be used for these projects. The maths ain't mathing.

All it does is allow fossil-fuel companies, Big Agriculture, corporations and governments to literally pay to pollute. It does very little to stop the pollution in the first place, but instead allows for them to continue business as usual and greenwash themselves. Even worse, these plans are set way too far into the future than what's actually needed. 'Net Zero by 2050' – as the UK government were forced to commit to – is too little, too late. 'Net Zero' won't save us. What we actually need is to have a real reduction in emissions, protection of existing carbon sinks *and* carbon-removal projects. We need to be aiming for Real Zero – or as close to that as possible – not Net Zero. That needs to be the focus – not just some creative accounting for the benefit of the elite.

The reason these false solutions cause so much harm is because they are not done with the intention of creating a climate-just world at all. They are only tunnel-visioned on certain types of emissions. When we focus on single-issue solutions like this, we allow space for the compromise of justice. We compromise the rights and liberation of peoples.

These are the times where we need to zoom out, look at the whole picture and make sure that we are seeing the whole of the climate and ecological crisis for all of its impacts. We have to have an awareness and an understanding of inequality, oppression, health, poverty and so much more that connects back to emissions.

Speaking to my friend Leo Cerda, Indigenous Land Defender and member of the Kichwa community of Serena in the Ecuadorian Amazon, provided an alternative to white environmentalism. Leo spoke with me about the idea that the future is Indigenous:

'We don't say that because it's a race. We say it because Indigenous Peoples have a value system that is in a close relationship to the earth.'[42]

It's this value system – the value systems of the communities all over the world who live in harmony with the rest of nature – that we must lean into if we are to survive. Rather than continuing into a future based on oppression, extraction, destruction and inequality, Indigenous futurism and Black futurism challenges us to have futures based on connection to nature, liberation and life affirmation.

Going beyond white environmentalism doesn't mean leaving all those racialised as white behind. It means leaving behind the system of whiteness, as we realise that it has been causing harm for too long. It means stepping into a new value system that leaves no one behind; a new value system that is healthy for all of us and for the planet. It means dismantling Euro-centric understandings of the climate crisis and seeing no stranger; recognising that each of us inherently valuable, related to each other and worthy of equal love and respect. It means understanding that the climate crisis is happening right now; that capitalism and white supremacy are oppressing and killing people all over the world. It means listening to and valuing Indigenous knowledge and value systems. It means understanding that academia and conservation are two specialities that were born from white supremacist ideals and thus they have proceeded to be violent against BIPOC communities. It means learning from and incorporating an understanding of different oppressive systems and their corresponding fights for liberation.

Going beyond white environmentalism means opening ourselves up to far more exciting and transformative visions for the future.

I use the word 'beyond' because white environmentalism is so limiting. It limits us to one understanding of the world. To go beyond this instead means no longer being limited by the false truths that white supremacy and capitalism have force-fed us. It means leaning into our radical imaginations. When we go beyond the visions of the world that whiteness has forced us all to internalise, we are opened up to so many more possibilities. We are liberated from the baggage of these systems. We can realise that the pillars of the world around us that we've been told are immutable, inevitable or 'just how things are' are all simply the result of the imaginations of the old, white men who created this world. These oppressive systems aren't inherently 'real'; they are only made real in their impacts when enough people believe in their reality. Once we understand this, we recognise how powerful our imaginations can be. We can realise the importance of fervently believing in our own radical imaginations for the world. We realise how huge the possibilities available to us are. To go beyond white environmentalism is to step into a world that we can – and will – transform.

Rather than being a distraction, racial justice offers us so many solutions. It strengthens our movements because it helps us to understand the climate crisis better. It helps us to draw those connections between these issues. When we make these connections, when we build coalitions between our respective struggles and work together, that's when we not only have a good chance of preventing the worst of climate breakdown, we also have the ability to create a truly liberated world. That benefits all of us.

As the American cultural theorist Fred Moten says so brilliantly on coalition:

'The coalition emerges out of your recognition that it's fucked up for you, in the same way that we've already recognised that it's fucked up for us. I don't need your help. I just need you to recognise that this shit is killing you, too, however much more softly, you stupid motherfucker, you know?'

The climate crisis will impact absolutely everyone on this earth in some way. It is a truly global threat. Solving it requires global collaboration. It requires heaps of different people doing different roles.

Considering that the modern climate movement began around the same time as the peak of the Civil Rights Movement, both in the US, I can't help but wonder what world we would be in now if the climate movement had reached out in coalition with movements for Black liberation from their inception.

Too many opportunities to build coalitions and create

stronger movements have been missed. As we touched on earlier, oppressed peoples of the not-so-distant past, such as Black communities in the south of the United States, and many Indigenous communities of the present, understand what it's like to live under and fight an existential threat. There is so much we can learn from these communities in resistance. We should be listening to these communities and learning from them and their tactics.

The climate crisis is connected to every single issue of exploitation and injustice in this world, so going to its roots and solving it with this knowledge can solve these issues too and build a stronger movement.

While my heart is broken for this world, it is also full of our human potential to create a better, radically transformed Earth, once we come together and build coalitions and bridges between our different struggles and move together towards our collective liberation. Coming together and building coalitions is the sort of thing that scares the status quo. It is powerful.

This is not a chance we have the luxury of wasting.

When I speak on coalition, I don't imagine that everything will be perfect. There will be disagreements. There will be differences in understanding. But my hope is that coming together under a shared goal of liberation will unite us in a way in which we can learn from each other in conversation and not only build a stronger movement together but weave each of our liberations into existing movements too. It's not an idealistic idea – we have seen this so many times before. From the Rainbow Coalitions between Black Panthers, Young Patriots and Young Lords in the late 1960s – which saw Fred Hampton, Chairman of the Chicago chapter of the Black Panther Party, unite unlikely allies of white working-class groups and Puerto Rican groups beyond their divisions against their common enemy – to the coalition displayed in the Oscar-nominated documentary *Crip Camp*.

This documentary tells the story of a summer camp for disabled children that then follows these same kids as adults leading the Disability Rights movement in the US. In the second half of the documentary, it shows one of the key actions by the movement: the 504 Sit-In. The documentary shows how this occupation of a US government building by the disability-rights activists was supported by Black Panthers and other liberation groups who provided food, joined the occupation and more. These other liberation groups joined this action in solidarity with their comrades fighting ableism as they recognised that no one is truly free until all of us are free. They realised that until all of us are safe, none of us are truly safe as there is no guarantee that we won't be next. They were aware of the interconnected nature of all of our liberation. They were aware that the oppression they faced and were fighting was tied to the oppression their siblings were fighting.

This sit-in – and so many other tactics and organising used – was eventually successful in achieving one of their key aims: the Disability Act. Of course, this win does not mean that the fight is over.

To see this clear example of the strength that comes from coalition building was so beautiful. It would be very difficult not to be brought to tears by it. It was a clear example of how, when we work together and build coalitions between our struggles, when we choose to be united, we can live in a small pocket of the liberated future we want, today. We can create that future today. A new world is very much within our reach – there are pockets of it being created all around us.

Phew. It's a lot to think about, right? If this is your first time understanding the colonial roots to the climate crisis, the fact that many 'solutions' proposed aren't really 'solutions' and the urgent need for reparations – that's OK. Take a moment to let yourself process everything you've just read. Don't get overwhelmed. Don't let the scale of the problem actually get in the way of you moving forward to work out what to do about it.

Whilst unlearning white environmentalism can feel like a lot, it's also so ridiculously exciting. How wonderful is it to know that we can go beyond the ways we have been told the world has to be? How exciting is it that our imaginations can go beyond these boundaries and think up new worlds?

Look, whiteness, white environmentalism and capitalism (which we'll be tackling in the next chapter) are all just ideas. They are the ideas of old white dudes from hundreds of years ago and they have only been made real because enough people have believed in them. If their imagination could create all this *gestures at millions of workers being exploited by corporations, colonialism and the world burning and flooding around us*, then our collective imaginations have the power to build something so much better. We just have to believe in them. This cannot be as good as it gets. We have to believe in the real possibility of the better world we are creating.

When I say belief in our imagination – an idea I will return to over and over again in this book – I don't mean just thinking about it. I don't mean just informing ourselves better. I don't mean just being passive. True belief in a new world requires us to take action to build it. It requires us to organise in our communities. It requires us to become active participants in building revolutionary change. As Indigenous climate justice organiser Big Wind River puts it, 'Don't just theorize, mobilize.'

The world as it is now is not set in stone. What the world will be – whether it continues to be based on oppressive principles of whiteness – is up to us.

4. DECONS-TRUCTING CAPITALISM

'We are left with a stark choice: allow climate disruption to change everything about our world, or change pretty much everything about our economy to avoid that fate. But we need to be very clear: because of our decades of collective denial, no gradual, incremental options are now available to us.'

—Naomi Klein, Canadian economist,
This Changes Everything: Capitalism vs. The Climate

'Environmentalism without class struggle is just gardening.'

—Chico Mendes,
Brazilian trade unionist and environmentalist

There is an assumption that climate disasters will happen all at once. That everything will fall apart on one specific day, collapsing into a ground-zero, D-Day apocalypse. The thought of this impending and approaching doom is scary. Either we avoid thinking about it because it feels inevitable and overwhelming, or we leap towards isolationism and individualism in anticipation of the day when we must abandon our connections to each other because 'everyone is out for themselves' as we fight our neighbours for food and water. This is the idea we have been sold of disaster; one of separation. We need to tell another story, one of coming together. One of a better world that is possible. In order to tell that new story – and make it a reality – we must challenge absolutely everything which leads us to an apocalyptic conclusion. We have to challenge capitalism.

That may sound like a daunting prospect, as capitalism is all many of us have ever known, and the idea of deconstructing it may feel utterly overwhelming. The very act of writing this chapter was the most daunting of the book.

I read endless books and papers, watched lectures, interviewed people and chatted to friends who study anti-capitalism full time. The more I read and watched, the more I was overwhelmed by how many alternatives to capitalism there are, and how much there is to know. But the deeper I got into my research, the more I realised that we can't expect everyone to read ten different books, watch dosens of talks, be able to understand academic papers or have hundreds of conversations in order to work towards a world beyond capitalism.

For a long time, I thought that in order to speak on climate and capitalism, I had to know everything and more. I think many of us have been made to feel that, unless we are an economist, we can't really challenge capitalism. That idea is completely untrue. Whilst educating ourselves is important, and engaging with the literature out there is helpful, it's just not reasonable to expect everyone to do it all in order to say anything about a system that is impacting all of our lives so intensely.

In this chapter, I aim to share a more accessible summary of different elements of the capitalism and climate conversation to equip you with the tools to feel more confident in understanding it and getting on with taking anti-capitalist action.

It would be absolutely impossible for me to explain the entirety of the capitalism problem and all the solutions available in one chapter. Many others have taken whole – or multiple – books to address this deeply complex and nuanced subject. To supplement this chapter, I encourage you to read the work of some of the campaigners, authors and academics mentioned throughout.

In a Q&A on Instagram, I was asked the big question of today: 'What can consumers do to stop the climate crisis?'

My response:

'You are not just a consumer. We are citizens. We are not just what we are made to be under capitalism. We are not limited by that. We are so much more. 'Consumers' cannot stop climate change because capitalism is not compatible with a climate-just world. But active citizens CAN. Movements CAN. WE CAN when we challenge and disrupt these systems, rather than limiting our power and actions to those which are within it.'[43]

Many will sell you false solutions to the climate crisis. I say this knowing that many will propagate those ideas with the best of intentions. Capitalism has an insidious habit of burrowing inside us and even making us believe liberation is a commodity. It makes us believe that it is impossible to escape from its clutches.

The reality is that we cannot consume our way out of a crisis that has been caused by excess consumption. Capitalism can't sell us liberation because it is the very cause of oppression for so many peoples.

Until we truly interrogate and dismantle the economic system that is currently forcing so many of us into unethical choices, and requires exploitation and oppression in order to enable extractions, especially in the Global South, our climate action will be inherently limited and flawed. We will continue to waste time fighting with each other over who is more perfect, when it is this system which is to blame, not the individual.

There's a lot of chat online and in climate spaces about capitalism. You've probably screamed into the void about the control it has on your life at some point, whether because of your dodgy landlord, ridiculous increases in bills or your pay cheque being constantly squeezed. But, at the same time, even in many climate-justice spaces, capitalism remains the elephant in the room. So what exactly *is* capitalism?

Capitalism is an economic system that requires and prioritises growth in capital (money) above all else. This growth is often equated to mean progress for humanity; more for all of us. That's a good thing, right? Unfortunately, as we will explore, that is not the case. Whilst capitalism is often described as offering greater freedom and individual choice to people, that is also a mischaracterisation. In short, capitalism is a system based on production for profit in private hands. It requires an imbalance in power between the workers – who create capital and value through their work – and the bosses who own the means of production. This imbalance in power happens at varying levels and scales, both within countries and globally.

Under capitalism, the aim of the economy is simply to create as much profit as possible, and it is therefore essential to extract as much value as possible from people and from ecosystems in order to feed the accumulation of capital. Corporations, usually with the willing assistance and protection of states, attempt to decrease costs wherever possible in order to maximise their profits. The costs being cut are often workers' wages, safety measures and policies that are in place to protect the environment. This profit for a few is produced via the exploitation of many. In a global sense, as imperialism has situated most extraction and manufacturing in Global South nations, most of these cuts happen there.

Capitalism requires endless growth – and not growth of things which serve society, but rather a continuous growth of capital, and the expansion of markets. To prop up its necessity to grow, it has to keep making items that none of us actually need and find a way of getting us to buy them, all so it can remain effective. Anything made, including things we do need, is deliberately made to break so that we are forced to buy a new replacement – a phenomenon referred to as planned obsolescence. Think about your phone, and the way in which the battery inevitably fails to hold enough charge to last you all day after a couple of years, or no longer supports necessary software updates. This dramatic decline in usability is not an accident – it's deliberately done to make a phone that could last for much longer feel increasingly more useless. Rather than encouraging or enabling repairs, the solution presented is simply to buy a completely new, upgraded model.

Capitalism causes a significant amount of waste. As a result of this, despite renewable capacity being the highest it's ever been, emissions are also at record highs and are ever increasing. These renewables, which should be replacing the need for fossil fuels, are instead being used to service completely unnecessary growth and production. I refuse to believe that this is the best economic system we can have. We have to refuse it, because it is quite literally leading us all to climate destruction unless we urgently change course.

The fast-fashion industry fully embodies this model. In pursuit of constant economic growth and increased profits, the production of garments in this industry is a race to the bottom; a race to make costs as low as possible and produce low-quality products to increase the number of purchases. Almost all production for this industry, from the farming of raw materials to the making of garments themselves, is situated in countries in the Global South in order to reduce costs and increase profits for the bosses of these companies in the Global North. Fast-fashion companies put constant pressure on their producers to be able to create more garments for less money, lest they lose their contracts to someone else who can. As a result, the working conditions in factories are made more and more unsafe for workers who are already paid poverty wages akin to modern slavery. The danger of this race to the bottom has sadly been displayed time and time again through the deaths of workers at their workplace, but it has never been seen more clearly than the collapse of the Rana Plaza factory in Bangladesh.

Rana Plaza was a factory that produced clothing for many major Western fast-fashion brands, from Primark to Mango, as well as luxury brands including Gucci and Prada. In the lead-up to the disaster, workers had complained to management about evident cracks in the walls of the building. Despite the obvious danger, management … workers they had to continue working, or lose one mon… pay. The building collapsed on the afternoon of 24 April 2013, killing over a thousand people and injuring a further 2,500. This catastrophic event remains the most deadly incident in the history of the fashion industry and yet, ten years on, lessons still fail to have been learned. Today, workers are still abused, and some even lose their lives in factories similar to Rana Plaza. Their safety is not prioritised, simply because it is not profitable. This obsession with profit, competition and growth is deadly.

Capitalism is younger than almost all major religions – organised around, dependent on and requiring perpetual growth. It's the first and only intrinsically expansionary system. If it doesn't grow, it collapses. It has to grow by 3 per cent every year, doubling the global economy every twenty years.[44] This is in complete contradiction to a finite planet, with planetary boundaries and finite resources. Capitalism does not value things like well-being or health or safety; it is only concerned with the pursued growth of capital. In this way, it fundamentally does not match up with the needs of people or the planet.

Capitalism is also inherently linked to race and white supremacy. Author and academic Emma Dabiri explains this in *What White People Can Do Next: From Allyship to Coalition*:

'One of the primary reasons behind the invention of race was to justify not just the exploitation of one group of people for the material benefit of another but to justify a new system, one we call capitalism. Slavery was the foundation of capitalism, capitalism was the foundation of modernity, and both built the infrastructure of the world we live in today. While capitalism exists, racism will continue. Even if black people achieved the impossible task of liberation under capitalism, another group would have to take their place. Exploitation and inequality are the operating logic of capitalism, in such an environment, not only will racism flourish, it will remain a prerequisite.'[45]

This capitalist system requires systems of oppression to deem the lives of some people disposable in the name of profit-making. In this way, capitalism is inherently linked to white supremacy, colonialism and slavery, which were necessary in order to build the capitalist economies of the Global North. This system of racially determined oppression and extraction has not ended. As a result, capitalism is frequently referred to as 'colonial capitalism' or 'racial capitalism'. Racism is actively maintained by structures, including states, in order to serve capitalism. This results in illness, disability and death by exploitation and oppression of those deemed 'less valuable' by whiteness, for the sake of profit.

In Global North countries like the United States and the UK, oppression and extraction of Black people continues via policing and the prison industrial complex (that is, the profit-driven relationship between the government and various businesses who build, manage, supply and service prisons), exploitative labour conditions and more. In the US alone, around 4,000 private companies profit from the prison system.[46] The prison system is extremely profitable for these companies, as it allows them to use prisoners for labour akin to slavery, given that the daily wage of incarcerated workers is only $0.86.[47] Therefore, they are incentivised to incarcerate more people whom society deems less valuable, simply to fulfil their desire for low-waged work and thereby maintain or increase their profits. Globally, rich countries have drained a whopping $152 trillion from the Global South – and thereby global-majority peoples – since 1960. This wealth transfer is the direct result of persistent extraction and exploitation from the Global South to the Global North, upheld and maintained through disproportionate control by a dominant Global North over international systems such as trade and debt.[48]

Racial capitalism is also linked to all other oppressive systems: patriarchy, ableism and, of course, class oppression. It thrives on hierarchy. Capitalism requires there to be someone at the bottom to exploit from. It requires inequity. We can never have collective liberation under a system like this.

Capitalism also requires systems of oppression to inhibit unity of the working classes. As Dabiri explains, race was invented to create division between oppressed peoples and prevent unity between enslaved Africans and the white working class. Whilst these two groups were both being oppressed in different ways, and to different extents, by the same people – the elite ruling class – this division was a significant barrier in stopping united opposition. Instead, oppressed peoples were pitted against each other and forced to see each other as the enemy rather than their true oppressors. This has persisted today, through the manifestations of racism in the messaging that any racially minoritised people coming to the UK will 'steal your job'; the scapegoating, violent immigration policies resulting in heightened precarity, and narratives of scarcity from politicians like Margaret Thatcher. Rather than seeing the global exploitation of the working class as good ground for building solidarity and connecting to each other, racism created by the ruling class has led many working-class people to fight each other instead. Whilst the majority of the world is still being exploited by the ruling class, we still lack the very necessary class unity needed to topple the system oppressing all of us.

To be clear, the blame for this lack of unity lies with the capitalist class (the bosses) who benefit from our division. They propagate these ideas and resist anything that challenges them because they are scared of the power of unity against them. These narratives and forces are one reason why there has been such a division between the environmental movement and trade-union movement. Presenting the situation we are in as being a battle of 'jobs versus the environment' has hindered progress from both sides. Two groups that have a shared foe – the fossil-fuel industry executives – have instead been pitted against each other. The fossil-fuel industry exploits both people and the planet in order to generate its wealth. From the people of the Niger Delta facing death, violence and pollution near Shell's sites of extraction to the working conditions of North Sea oil workers, the exploitation of people goes hand in hand with the exploitation of the planet. The climate movement has too often failed to make these connections. As we will discuss in more depth in the next chapter, a Just Transition is a concept that aims to repair the rift between the labour and climate movements, building a coalition that is strong enough to tackle the companies and economic system profiting from both climate breakdown and worker exploitation. This is so heavily resisted, as the ruling class understands that a united global majority, strong unions, coalition and general strikes have the power to take them down.

Whilst this should all be enough for us to demand something new, that is not the limit to the problems with capitalism. As we have already touched on, capitalism and the planet are at odds with each other. As economist Naomi Klein put it in *This Changes Everything*:

'What the climate needs to avoid collapse is a contraction in humanity's use of resources; what our economic model demands to avoid collapse is unfettered expansion. Only one of those sets of rules can be changed, and it's not the laws of nature.'[49]

It is clear that current consumption levels in the Global North are incompatible with life on this planet. It currently takes the earth a whole year and eight months to regenerate the resources we currently consume, globally, in just a year. How humanity is currently operating does not match up with what we need in order to collectively survive for the long term. Rather than continuing to try and fit the round peg that is a liveable planet into the square hole that is capitalism, we should be concentrating our attention on creating and building a new economic system that works for both people and the planet.

So often, to even suggest that we should have an alternative economic system is met with incredulous responses. There is this idea that there is nothing we can do to change this system. Sci-fi author Ursula Le Guin challenges this notion, saying:

'We live in capitalism. Its power seems inescapable. So did the divine right of kings. Any human power can be resisted and changed by human beings. Resistance and change often begin in art, and very often in our art, the art of words.'[50]

So, we must challenge capitalism in all the ways possible to us. I'm a strong believer in the fact that you don't have to have a solution in order to raise awareness of a problem. As a medic, I know that it's harder to begin healing if we don't even know that there's an injury. That being said, I do believe we need to have some sort of idea of what we're fighting for, as well as what we're fighting against.

When I first got involved with climate activism, I had absolutely no clue about economic systems and how they work. I probably couldn't even tell you what capitalism was. In many ways, I started off as a neoliberal green capitalist,††† as I just focused on individual actions and making better choices within the system to improve it, rather than challenging it, without even knowing what the term 'neoliberal green capitalist' meant. I was trying to 'do good', but I did so by following mainstream advice. I'd talk about changing consumption habits and voting with your dollar/ pound/currency – the idea that we can simply usher or vote in a better world by allocating our money to better choices through our purchases, thus voting these choices in – without fundamentally interrogating capitalism or understanding it. In trying to do good, I was actually unknowingly propping up a harmful system and giving it space to adapt and remain relevant for the long term. Looking back, I realise now that, whilst there can be some truth in the 'voting with your dollar' idea, it's inherently limited. Simply speaking, if you have more dollars, you get more votes. I don't believe that we should have a system where those who benefit most from upholding an unequal system – and therefore have the most dollars or votes – get to choose what sticks around.

As we discussed in the previous chapter, green capitalism, which simply acts to replace everything we currently consume with 'green' alternatives, does not offer material

††† I'm going to dive a bit more into the impact of neoliberalism on the individual in Chapter 9. Don't worry if you don't know what this means yet!

improvements to the lives of the people currently struggling to survive today. The climate crisis, despite being the biggest and most wide-reaching, is not the only crisis we are experiencing. We have a cost of living crisis, poverty, white supremacy and racism, millions of displaced and unhoused people existing at the same time as billionaires with obscene levels of wealth. Green capitalism does not tackle any of these crises. Not a single one. In fact, it sustains them.

Whilst I challenge the 'voting with your dollar approach' and individualist perfectionism, this doesn't necessarily mean I reject the need for any individual lifestyle change whatsoever. One of the big debates in the environmental movement asks whether we should be focused on individual lifestyle changes or systemic change. I believe this is a false debate; what we really need is for both to take place. Making our climate action reliant on incremental, individual lifestyle changes ignores the reality of the fact that many of the biggest contributions to climate change from lifestyles are things that individuals simply cannot 'opt out' from. To focus on this just breeds unhelpful perfectionism. The individualisation of responsibility – as we have touched on in the previous chapters – misallocates blame, and to make a perfectly eco-friendly lifestyle a prerequisite to take climate action is counterproductive to our cause. Moreover, this individualisation of responsibility assumes an agency which frankly isn't there for most people.

However, we can't solely focus on changing the systems whilst keeping our lifestyles and behaviours the same. The answer is not to do nothing, but to use our collective power. Some boycotts have been shown to create sufficient pressures needed for transformational change to be possible, and they can be an important tactic. Fast fashion is a key area where both boycotts and behaviour change to reduce consumption are of vital importance for both the planet and solidarity with the exploited workers in the industry. Moreover, for us to truly tackle emissions, those of us in the Global North need to take on more climate-friendly behaviours. In the UK, even if we do manage to switch the entire power supply to renewable energy by 2050, as is the current government's plan, our current energy demand (that is, the energy we use) is so huge that we wouldn't have enough renewables to meet that demand. This isn't to say that we need fossil fuels for ever, but rather that, whilst we scale up renewables and switch the supply, we also need to reduce energy consumption or demand. Some of that must come from behaviour change. But many of these behaviour changes are only made possible – or available to the masses – if there is infrastructure implemented to enable those changes and to reduce the growth obsession that makes the energy demand so vast.

Often, this need to reduce our consumption of energy has been understood as climate activists asking all of us – even those who are currently struggling with barely enough – to make huge sacrifices and try to live with less. This is a mischaracterisation. The need to 'live with less' is true only for the richest in the population who are currently overconsuming, rather than the majority of the population who are already struggling to survive with what they have.

Under capitalism, we are producing more than enough food to feed everyone on Earth, yet there are billions of people who are starving. We have amazing technologies in healthcare, but the majority of the world can't access them. We have millions of homes sitting empty whilst millions are unhoused. Rather than all of these resources being directed by human or planetary need, they are only directed by profits.

It's because of this misdirection of resources that capitalism creates artificial scarcity. I began this chapter with the depiction of an apocalyptic future where we must fight each other for scarce resources. This might be an idea of the future you have had too. We are led to this conclusion because many of us are tricked into believing that we are already living in a world with insufficient resources to go around, when in actuality the resources that do exist are simply being hoarded by the wealthy. This is another key area where capitalism requires systems of oppression. As well as deeming people's lives less worthy in order to facilitate exploitation, capitalism must also deem huge segments of the population undeserving of resources, support and compassion in order to justify this false scarcity.

How many times have we been told in the UK that 'benefits scroungers' are causing the collapse of our public services, while tax breaks for bankers go unquestioned? How many times are 'migrant hotels' (in reality violent detention centres without adequate access to food, education or healthcare) blamed for poverty in the UK, rather than the massive rise in shareholder payouts and bosses' pay? To meet everyone's needs, we must move away from the capitalist system which pits us against each other as isolated individuals, and demands we fight over scraps, whilst the billionaires and the corporates bleed us and our planet dry. To move away from scarcity for the majority, we must find a fairer way of distributing resources. As Ruth Wilson-Gilmore, abolitionist and prison scholar, said in a recent interview, 'Nobody anywhere at any time should lack for food, shelter, healthcare, education, clean water – the kinds of things that we can only produce if we produce them together'.[51]

This idea of false scarcity is enhanced by the fact that capitalism also manipulates us to consume much more than we need. It perpetuates the false illusion that buying more stuff will make us happier and more connected to and accepted by our peers. Instead of unnecessary consumption on a background of scarcity, a climate-justice-based economy could provide *more* of the things that we actually need and want for survival and happiness for the majority of the population, not only in the UK and the Global North, but all over the world. All of our lives would be improved if we no longer had to rely on buying things to attend to our emotional health, and rather prioritised an economy that exists to centre human need, connection to each other and experiences. This is an inherently decolonial project, as a climate-just economy would see the struggle for better living conditions as a global, anti-imperial project. It would address the debts owed to nations who have currently and historically been deliberately oppressed and prevented from developing, as they were constantly being robbed and extorted by countries in the core. It would also increase the material living conditions of those currently living precariously in the Global North.

Rather than all of us being required to have 'less', we could instead have more: warmer homes, better healthcare, more free time and shorter work weeks, accessible and healthier food, universal basic income, lower energy bills. Things like the insulation of homes, heat pumps, cycle lanes, and better and cheaper public transport are all provisions that would reduce our overall consumption of energy but that would actually provide more in the sense of well-being for all of us. Right now, these things would require government intervention to decentralise our energy system out of the control of capitalist companies and into the hands of local communities, giving the decision-making power to them and implementing the large-scale infrastructure changes needed.

The movement and theory behind scaling down growth and consumption in the Global North, away from capitalism and towards a world that is big enough for us all, is called degrowth. You may not be convinced by it yet, and perhaps you're still holding on to the idea that to reduce consumption and move away from capitalism would force us all to return to the Stone Age? You might be thinking that these are nice ideas, but they are perhaps unrealistic.

A study titled 'Providing decent living with minimum energy: A global scenario' worked to address that exact question. In this study, authors Joel Millward-Hopkins, Julia K. Steinberger, Narasimha D. Rao and Yannick Oswald modelled what a global reduction of current energy consumption by 60 per cent could look like by 2050. They found that not only is this possible, but it can be done whilst maintaining a high quality of life for every single person on earth. This 60 per cent reduction was not equal across all nations. To account for climate debt, for high historical and present emitters like the US, the reduction of emissions modelled was as much as 95 per cent. Even with this huge reduction in emissions – which would allow for our collective survival in the face of this climate crisis and improvement of living conditions for billions – the lifestyles of every person on earth would be decent ones, with universal healthcare, air-conditioned homes, computers and safe housing. This was done accounting for a population of almost *ten billion*. This reduction in consumption would require us to simply return to energy-usage levels of the 1960s, efficiently using the technology we have available to us now, rather than returning us to the Stone Age. Growth simply does not have to happen for people in richer countries to live well.

These aren't simply ideas, or even just studies. There are plans like the Tricontinental's *A Plan To Save The Planet* and the People's Green New Deal which are working on how to move us away from capitalism, exploitation, unfettered growth and planetary destruction and towards an economy that really works for everyone. These plans are people- and, vitally, planet-focused rather than profit-focused.

Whilst it's so important that we don't let go of the fight for human rights and dignity for all in our struggle for a climate-compatible economy, it's simultaneously vital that we don't leave behind climate demands in the call for a more equitable economy. Unfortunately, whilst less harmful than capitalism, socialism – an alternative to capitalism which centres the economy on people's needs rather than profit – does not necessarily eliminate or prevent environmental destruction. It is very possible for socialist economies to still be based on climate-destroying extractivist industries. We must advocate for a combination of eco-socialism with degrowth instead; an economy that does not require exploitation of the planet or the many, whilst also meeting the needs of all people on this Earth.

An attempt at creating eco-socialism can be seen by Evo Morales's first MAS (Movement Towards Socialism) administration in Bolivia in the early 2000s. Establishing Bolivia as a plurinational state was a move by MAS to recognise the autonomy of Indigenous communities in pursuit of an Indigenous-led socialism. Morales made clear declarations to protect the environment, which his administration claimed both nationally and on the global stage. In many ways, this was realised through a redistribution of Bolivia's wealth from a huge tax on private fossil-fuel companies to the people, in the form of direct payments and social programmes, and enshrining protection of Pachamama (Mother Nature) into law. Moreover, the convening of over one hundred countries in Cochabamba to create an ambitious climate agenda that addressed climate debt, colonialism and imperialism brought the world along with Morales's vision. However, fully realising eco-socialism has not yet been a full possibility for Bolivia. Due to the legacy of colonialism working to underdevelop Bolivia – making it the poorest country in South America when Morales was first elected – during his first presidency, Morales was forced into a choice between the urgent need to improve living standards and retaining his environmental beliefs. In proposing plans to build highways through the protected Indigenous land in the TIPNIS (Territorio Indígena y Parque Nacional Isiboro Secure) national park to open the country to more trade, he was sacrificing the same primary forests he had vowed to protect and the Indigenous communities and cosmologies he claimed to represent. These extractivist actions were met with huge Indigenous resistance, including from Morales's own Aymaran Indigenous community.

For Morales's Bolivia, fully realising eco-socialism was inhibited in part due to the historic obstacles left by colonial extraction and existing imperialism. In order to fully realise eco-socialism, a transfer of wealth back to Bolivia from the colonist nations who grew at their expense is needed to fund this transition.

Richer nations who have historically caused this climate crisis have both the capacity and responsibility to transition their economies, whilst also transferring wealth back to countries like Bolivia. This transfer of wealth could enable Global South countries to 'develop' on their own terms, beyond extractivism. Our survival globally is interconnected.

Those of us in these countries must build power to create a fairer, better economy which attends to climate debts.

A Plan To Save The Planet maps out what this could look like, tackling medical, money and food apartheid to direct our world away from capitalism and destruction and towards a more equitable and safe world with an economy free from the control of a handful of companies and governments. Created by a bunch of research institutes from all over the world in the wake of the COVID-19 pandemic, this plan translates ideas of a liberated world into how we can practically create it and what is required. From debt cancellation to advancing a people's vaccine for COVID and from redistributing land to working to eliminate violence against women and LGBTQ+ people, the *Plan* recognises that to tackle capitalism in pursuit of a liveable future is to also tackle the oppressive systems from which our multiplicity of crises arise. I really encourage you to do some research and read through the plan itself, as it has brought me a lot of hope.

We really must remember that this work can't only get us out of the acute threat of the climate crisis, but rather, it should be about tackling all forms of crisis and preventing more from occurring. It should be about transformation rather than preservation.

Like everything in this world, capitalism is just a concept. It's an idea which has been made real by enough people believing in it and acting on it. You, reading this book, have probably attributed permanence to this idea and this system. I have too. It's impossible not to when it impacts pretty much every aspect of our lives and whether we are able to live. I'm not going to suggest here that you can escape capitalism by simply deciding to no longer believe in it. What I am saying, and what American political activist and scholar Angela Davis said so well in her lecture 'How Does Change Happen?', is the following: 'We must not attribute any permanency to that which is, simply because it is.'[52]

Why? Because if we never challenge capitalism, then we'll be stuck with it.

Rather than painting capitalism green, we must challenge the system itself. There is often a fear around challenging our existing capitalist structure, as many folks don't know what else is out there. It can seem like the only options available to us are capitalism or communism. On the latter, most of what we've been sold are stories of seemingly more oppressive communist states like the USSR. Dictatorships have been presented to the masses as the only alternative to capitalism. That doesn't seem very appealing. In response to this, many of us have internalised Margaret Thatcher's doctrine that 'there is no alternative'.

Instead of uniting against the capitalist system and class, many instead go to extreme lengths to defend the same system that is oppressing them. We are all far closer to homelessness than to ever becoming a billionaire, so defending the latter at the expense of the former only works to benefit the capitalist elites and harm the rest of us. Yet so many people are made to believe that they have more of a chance of one day joining the billionaire class or 1 per cent elite than of achieving an economy that works for all of us – even though that chance of extreme wealth is almost impossible. Rather than fighting for that better world, they choose to protect the right of the 1 per cent to exploit and overconsume, just in case there is an opportunity to one day step into that world. These actions or aspirations don't come from a place of wishing exploitation on others, but instead from one of truly feeling that this is the only choice that will offer protection and stability.

This is why we need a climate movement that presents a better option than the one we have now. We need a climate movement that understands oppression as it exists now and offers solutions that would actually change the material conditions of the people most oppressed in society. We need to change the narrative away from the aspirational meritocracy of being able to one day go from oppressed to oppressor towards a vision of a world where we have left oppression behind. That requires class struggle to be central to climate struggle. That is how we win this.

Why are we holding on to a system that has historically and presently caused so much harm, and is leading to our collective destruction? Do we not believe that we deserve, and can have, better?

What has been so exciting in all of this research is discovering how many alternatives there are out there. All of these alternatives offer a world that is *better*. That's doubly exciting because, rather than one solution, or one system to replace capitalism, we need a multiplicity of systems and futures to fit different contexts. And – this is really important – we need to open our minds up to imagine the vast possibilities out there.

For far too long, the climate movement has tried to scare, inform or guilt people into action. None of this has been effective enough.

Fear isn't a great motivator – it can lead us into isolationist and oppressive, separatist politics. The right loves it. More than that, it doesn't work for the long term. As Octavia E. Butler wrote in her novel *The Parable of The Sower*, 'It's harder to scare them a second time, harder to teach them, harder to win back their trust.'[53]

Bombarding people with information isn't enough – it's far too easy to get desensitised and not everyone has the time or ability to understand the complexities of climate science or economic theory. Guilt can lead to a blame game and giving up. What we really need is motivation. Hope. In illustrating that the climate crisis is a product of capitalism, we can show that, by tackling the climate crisis, we can also tackle the roots of a system that is harming all of us. We can provide a future free from exploitation, from poor working conditions, material insecurity and inequality. This can unite us.

Rather than just providing fear, knowledge or guilt, we can offer increases in the material conditions of people's lives. As well as stopping a future crisis from happening, we could also tackle the multiplicity of crises that the majority of people are facing today, with astronomical increases in the cost of living, the majority of lives being spent working for very little pay, and the lack of access to so many things that are necessary in order to live a life in dignity, safety and joy. In tackling the climate crisis and capitalism together, we are offering a truly liberated future for all of us. That's pretty exciting.

To do this requires the climate movement – and every single one of us – to really support those movements that are taking down the capitalist class brick by brick. It means supporting strike funds, joining and participating in trade unions and incorporating the tactics that have historically made wins against the capitalist system into our organising. It's so much more than lifestyle switches. It's transformational, material changes for the majority of people that we need to see.

What can you do on an individual level? Join a union; contribute to strike funds; help make general strikes happen;[‡‡‡] allow yourself to imagine a multiplicity of futures and work out how to move towards them. Advocate for climate debt to be addressed and for existing Global South debt to be cancelled so that there can be a global transition away from imperialism. Get involved in work that is directed at tackling the producing class – the bosses and titans of industry – and work to take these corporations down. Call out their greenwashing to take down their social licences – a topic we will be covering in the next chapter. And importantly, build support and power in our communities and through our political systems so that the future we need can be won by the masses. We must build widespread support for an eco-socialist, post-growth future.

The climate crisis makes the fight against capitalism more urgent than ever. This fight is inherently political. There are a lot of people with a lot of power who are doing all that they can to maintain the capitalist system. As I write this, the Conservative government in the UK is putting in legislation to make striking illegal, and the main opposition party, Labour, refused to say they would repeal these laws. We cannot let them do this. We need to build a movement against capitalism that has enough power to take it on. Great changes have happened in the past and have been won by the people. We can – and will – do it again.

‡‡‡ A general strike happens when workers from most or all industries work together to organise to strike at the same time. The power this can have against the capitalist system is immense. It shows how the power to keep a country and society running is truly with the workers and the people, not the bosses.

5.
IN DENIAL MUCH? THE FOSSIL-FUEL INDUSTRY

A note for this chapter: I owe the vast majority of what I know about greenwashing and climate denial from the work of the brilliant investigative journalist Amy Weestervelt. Drilled: A True Crime Podcast About Climate Change, *hosted and created by Weestervelt, is an absolutely essential listen for everyone. Listening to seasons one and three of the show is a great way to supplement the information provided in this chapter. It will really piss you off in the best way. We need to get a lot angrier with fossil-fuel companies for what they have done and are continuing to do.*

In October 2021, a group made up of my friends, fellow activists and Stop Cambo campaigners organised a successful action against the platforming of Royal Dutch Shell's CEO, Ben van Beurden, by TED Countdown in Edinburgh. TED had invited van Beurden to speak on stage with Costa Rican diplomat Christiana Figueres and Chris James from 'investor activist organization' Engine No.1 on a panel about 'Reducing'. This panel came at the same time as Shell were attempting to approve the massive Cambo oil field in the nearby North Sea, mere months after this same company appealed a court ruling in The Hague which had instructed them to reduce their worldwide emissions by 45 per cent by 2030, and mere weeks before the twenty-sixth anniversary of the execution of nine Nigerian activists who were killed by the state for campaigning against Shell's exploitation of the Ogoni land. As a company that continues to profit from the proliferation of the climate crisis, funds climate denial and delay and has committed neo-colonial violence, it should never be platformed or welcomed in climate spaces.

Three days before the conference was set to start, I and a couple of my friends who had been invited found out about the panel. I had already declined my invitation to attend TED Countdown for a number of reasons – it seemed to me to be a very reformist, green-capitalist event where no local organisers and few MAPA (Most Affected People and Areas) activists were invited. However, whether I was attending or not, there was no chance that Shell's CEO would speak on a panel in my home city without being challenged.

You might be wondering why anyone would think it acceptable for a fossil-fuel company – the ones causing the destruction – to be welcomed at spaces that say they're championing climate justice. Or, perhaps you're thinking, *well, how they act will have a huge impact on our future, shouldn't we want them on board?*

Fossil-fuel companies have been obsessed with being associated with just about anything that isn't what they actually do – destroying the planet – for decades. According to their greenwashed marketing campaigns, their sponsorship of the arts,[§§§] museums[****] and their presence at climate conferences and events, you'd be forgiven for thinking that they're mostly renewable energy companies with good consciences. Fossil-fuel companies are truly the original catfishers. All of this is part of a deceptive marketing campaign that began with the same people behind marketing both Big Tobacco and the Third Reich (yes, you read that right). To fully understand all of this, we're going to have to dive into the concept of a 'social licence' and a brief history of climate denial and greenwashing.

The key thing to understand is that fossil-fuel companies – and yes, I really do mean all of them – simply do not care one ounce about tackling the climate crisis. Let me say that again – they do not care. They don't have consciences because they aren't people – they're corporations. They exist to make as much profit as possible for their shareholders. Even if the US constitution views corporations as having the same rights as people, they fundamentally aren't.

Whatever their social-media accounts may say, whatever their web pages say, no matter how many climate conferences they attend, all of these actions are being carried out for one thing and one thing only: to allow them to exist for as long as possible and to make as much profit as possible. These actions – the fossil-fuel industry's catfishing tactics – have been named 'greenwashing'.

---

§§§ The Royal Ballet and the National Portrait Gallery in the UK.

**** The Science Museum chose fossil-fuel giants Adani coal and Royal Dutch Shell as sponsors for climate exhibits. The Science Museum was my favourite place to visit growing up, so this one cut hard.

Greenwashing is defined as the actions taken by a company in order to present itself as more climate-friendly than it actually is. This process is not limited to fossil-fuel companies, as many others also participate. In response to campaigners pointing out the damaging impact of fast fashion on the planet, for instance, the clothing brand H&M created a 'conscious' range made of organic cotton, recycled plastic and other so-called sustainable materials. Meanwhile, they continued producing staggering numbers of garments – an estimated 3 billion per year. This is a classic example of greenwashing in action.

Greenwashing is the tactic or process used by companies in order to obtain a social licence – that is, the idea that we collectively allow the existence of certain industries and companies because we deem them to be acceptable, worthy or necessary. Greenwashing is so dangerous because it allows harmful and violent companies to continue to exist for longer.

Understanding what a social licence is – and why so many climate-wrecking corporations are completely obsessed with it – is absolutely essential. We need to understand what it is and why it's so important, so that we don't contribute to it.

As a collective, we do things we sometimes don't even realise we're doing. If enough of us think, whether actively or passively, that a company isn't that bad, is even good, or, worse, necessary, then we bestow upon them a social licence. It's a pass that means that governments will continue to subsidise these companies – subsidies that amount to a ridiculous eleven million dollars per minute, globally, for the fossil fuel industry alone. It's a pass that allows these fossil fuel companies to have hundreds of lobbyists attending UN climate conferences – over six hundred of them were at COP27. These lobbyists have worked to successfully prevent any agreement on fossil-fuel phase-outs from being present in any global climate agreement thus far – including the Paris Agreement. Whilst this pass isn't physical or tangible, the consequences of this social licence are very, very real and we all need to be aware of it.

These companies know that what they're doing is destroying the planet, and they know that more of us are starting to recognise that too. Despite their best efforts to deny it – and my god, did they try their hardest to bury the science – the reality of climate change is now accepted by governments, industry and the public.

So how did we end up here? It's time for a (very) brief history of climate denial.

Back in the 1970s, Exxon, an American multinational oil and gas corporation, set up their own research centre focused on energy. Wanting to be at the forefront of energy research – on nuclear, solar and, of course, fossil fuels – they hired some of the best scientists in the field and brought them together. A huge focus of the research was on climate change, which at the time was a non-partisan issue. Ed Garvey, one of the scientists who worked for Exxon during this time, said the following about their work:

'The issue was not, were we going to have a problem? The issue was simply, how soon and how fast and how bad was it going to be? Not if. Nobody at Exxon when I was there was discussing that. It was just OK, how fast is it going to come? Can we do something about it? How bad is it going to be and when is it going to get here? But not if.'[54]

This research by Exxon led to the creation of some of the most advanced modelling systems of the time to understand climate change. They conducted research into how burning fossil fuels was contributing to the climate crisis that would completely devastate the planet. So much of what we are seeing now was predicted then. At the time, Exxon was a huge company with many different branches, including renewable-energy branches, and as a result, many of the scientists working on research believed that Exxon truly was an energy company rather than solely being a fossil-fuel company and that, given the unequivocal data they had on the climate crisis, they would change course immediately, push for a full transition away from fossil fuels and plunge their profits into renewable investments. This was in the 1980s. As we know now, they didn't do that. If they had done, we would be living in a vastly different world than we are now.

Their own scientists begged Exxon to release this information publicly and get governments to take action. Instead, they did the opposite. They slashed funding and closed their research centres, buried the information and hired the best PR folks they could find – the very same people who created health-impact-denying propaganda for Big Tobacco – to create one of the biggest social-influence campaigns the world has ever seen: a mass climate-denial programme. As Amy Westervelt describes on her podcast *Drilled*, they 'began to wage an informational war on climate science'. They understood early on that if climate change was going to become a war over knowledge, then they would be the ones to control that information from the beginning. This programme was so successful that a 2019 report by Yale found that 32 per cent of Americans still thought that global warming is due mostly to natural changes in the environment. That's despite all of the IPCC reports, protests and campaigns.[55]

Once Exxon was no longer winning the denial-war, they

adapted their campaign to delay. They funded adverts which popularised individualised responsibility through the concept of an individual carbon footprint. They began sponsoring cultural institutions and presenting themselves as renewable-energy companies, in spite of only 2 per cent of their operations being renewables whilst the remaining 98 per cent are all still fossil fuels. This still persists today and is a big reason – if not the commanding reason – why fossil fuels are still being extracted and burned at scales that are fundamentally incompatible with sustaining life on this planet.

Today, they're still working on their delay strategy. Make no mistake, even though it looks different from denial, it is equally as deadly. Both climate delay and climate denial will lead us to the same result: extinction. The only thing that can save us is real climate action: beginning a rapid, just transition to full decarbonisation immediately.

Climate delay looks like the obvious changing policy to further push back deadlines for phasing out fossil fuels, but there are also more sinister manifestations. There's the increasing focus on false solutions that we addressed earlier. By promoting and making their current emissions targets reliant on technologies like carbon-capture and storage, companies and governments are trying to find creative ways to allow them to continue to keep burning fossil fuels for longer and to put more and more polluting gases into our atmosphere.

It's often said that fossil-fuels companies aren't taking climate change seriously. But they have in fact been taking it far more seriously than almost any other institution since they found out how devastating their own products were in the 1980s. They have taken climate change so seriously that they have spent billions of dollars on delaying progress and action. If they really thought it was a hoax, would they be trying so hard to fight it? They are putting all this effort in because they *do* see this crisis as serious, but not in terms of how it will impact people. Instead, they're concerned solely with how it will impact their profits.

After all of this, it's clear that fossil-fuel companies have not only taken climate change seriously, but that they know how bad the climate crisis is and will continue to be. They have known this in more detail and for longer than almost any other industry or government in the world. They have known since the 1980s that their production is killing the planet and could lead to our extinction and that did not stop them. It did not stop them then, and it's most definitely not stopping them now.

This is why I believe that engaging with these companies, urging or cajoling them to change by telling them the climate science, or how bad things are and will get, is a waste of our time. They already know all of this! Our efforts should not be directed towards appealing to their non-existent conscience. Instead, our efforts should be towards disrupting them at every single opportunity and making their climate-destroying activities impossible. Taking them down by taking away their social licence, their subsidies, and their investors. We cannot trust them not to be completely appalling. Even if they switch all of their operations to renewable energy, I still would not trust them. They have shown us time and time again that they will always choose the path of most exploitation. We do not need them.

The focus of this chapter is on the fossil-fuel bad guys, but this denial campaign was more than just them. The media has played – and continues to play – a huge role in delaying and preventing adequate action on climate change.

Some of this comes from working directly with the fossil-fuel industry to disseminate misinformation through sponsored advertorials. These advertorials are articles presented as editorials, when in fact they are insidiously sponsored pieces written by and for the fossil-fuel industry. The *Washington Post* has published a bunch of these articles by the American Petroleum Institute (API) with headlines boldly reading, 'Why Pipelines and Production are pathways to progress' and 'Low- and no-carbon future starts with natural gas', with the 'partner content' disclaimer only visible to those who read the small print.[††††]

The media's climate denial also has a lot to do with the fact that five billionaires own 80 per cent of the UK media. A similar trend is seen all over the world. These billionaires influence what is and is not reported on. They influence the way an issue is talked about. They create false 'two-sides' arguments, presenting climate change as a debate with two equal sides, and undermining the very serious reality. They have deliberately and systematically confused the public on the seriousness of this issue, and they continue to do so. They do all of this because it benefits them. They do it because they don't want the public to challenge the aviation industry, the fossil-fuel industry or the obscenely rich billionaire class. They thrive on inequality and inequity: they thrive on capitalism. They know that in tackling the climate crisis, we have to also tackle capitalism. They don't want that. So, they do everything they can to spread misinformation and prevent the public from rising up to create a better society for the

†††† You can have a look at the *Post*'s shameless advertorials here: https://www.washingtonpost.com/creativegroup/sponsor/api/

majority of people.

Whilst it may seem that the war being fought here is one of awareness or knowledge, it's important that we understand that that's not all it is. It is not just about social licences, or what the public knows or does not know about climate change. It's not just about what is understood by most people. It's about power. It's about these fossil-fuel companies and billionaires buying politicians and entire political parties through donations. It's about lobbying. We must be careful here not to just see this as an awareness or information war. It's about far more than that.

At the TED Countdown conference in Edinburgh, thanks to a bunch of organising by many youth activists behind the scenes, we were able to get Stop Cambo activist Lauren MacDonald onto the panel that Shell's CEO Ben van Beurden was set to speak on. Whilst we hadn't been granted our request for him to be removed from the event completely, we weren't going to stop there. We weren't going to allow a 'respectable' panel about climate change to happen with one of the main producers of this crisis participating. On the panel, Lauren delivered a powerful speech calling out Shell and van Beurden in front of the world. You can find the full clip on TED.com – hilariously and oxymoronically titled 'Decarbonising Fossil Fuels'. It can also be seen on Lauren's Instagram account, @laurenthesunflower. Here is some of what she said:

'Mr van Beurden, I just want to start by saying that you should be absolutely ashamed of yourself for the devastation you have caused to communities all over the world. Already, you are responsible for so much death and suffering.

I'm not even going to appeal to you to change, because

that would be a wasted opportunity. What I do want to say is that every single day that you fail to stop making evil decisions is a day that the death toll of the climate crisis rises. You are one of the most responsible people for this crisis in the world, and in my view that makes you one of the most evil people in the world. . . Disproportionately, in the Global South, so many people are already dying due to issues related to the climate crisis such as pollution, extreme heat and weather-related disasters. This is not an abstract issue and you [van Beurden] are directly responsible for those deaths.'[56]

Lauren then asked Ben van Beurden whether – in the face of all of the science on the climate crisis – Shell would still be appealing the recent court ruling in the Netherlands? It was a yes or no question, and van Beurden failed to provide one of those responses.

Lauren responded to his attempt at avoiding the question by saying:

'I hope that you know that we will never forget what you have done, what Shell has done. I hope you know that as the climate crisis gets more and more deadly, you will be to blame. I will not be sharing this podium with you any more . . . I do not agree with Shell being given this platform.'[57]

Youth activists involved with organising the action and attendees left, chanting 'Don't just watch us, join us'. I wasn't there in person, but watching it on the livestream, it was one of the most moving actions I've ever seen. I am so ridiculously proud of every single person involved, especially my dear friend Lauren for having the bravery to challenge van Beurden on stage at such short notice.

The impact of this action sent a clear message that fossil-fuel companies are not – and should not ever – be welcome in climate spaces. It made a huge contribution towards Shell being forced to drop their investment in the Cambo oil field just a couple of months later, leading to the other investor, Siccar Point Energy, being forced to indefinitely pause the project. If Cambo had been extracted from, and the oil burned, it would have created emissions equivalent to ten times the annual emissions of Scotland. Stopping this field – and any field – from being extracted will result in many future lives being saved or made safer. This historic win for the climate was heralded as a 'death knell' for big North Sea oil and gas projects by industry insiders – who clearly identified resistance by activists as the causation.

Many other actions have been and are taken every day to resist fossil-fuel companies' greenwashing tactics. Groups like BP or Not BP in the UK have been using a diversity of tactics, including direct action, to end oil sponsorships of cultural institutions for over ten years. These concerted actions have resulted in sixteen cultural institutions, including the Tate, the Southbank Centre, the BFI, the Royal Shakespeare Company and the British Film Institute, removing sponsorships from oil companies like Shell and BP. Fossil Free London is a group which exists to constantly challenge fossil-fuel companies in England's capital city. Campaigns and groups like these are so important. We need to get to the point where fossil-fuel companies are so detestable that no institution wants to associate with them. We need to get to a point where, as a society, we collectively come together to say that these violent, destructive, neocolonialist companies should not exist and are not necessary.

This really matters. Currently, a huge part of the continued existence of fossil-fuel companies is down to the fact that they have a social licence. This social licence allows politicians who advocate for this industry to continue to get elected. These companies receive billions in public money in the form of subsidies or tax breaks every day, the subsidies equating to $11 million every minute.[58] Our public money, which should be used for public good, is instead being used to prop up an industry that is leading us towards extinction. We all need to act to stop this.

Many of us are. Thanks to huge amounts of work by journalists like Amy Westervelt, action groups like Culture Unstained, NGOs like Friends of the Earth, direct opposition at the sites of extraction by Indigenous and other frontline communities all over the world, and grassroots groups like Fossil Free London, the general public are gaining more of an understanding of the violent reality of the fossil-fuel industry and are showing opposition. The Stop Cambo campaign was a key point in history for the climate movement in the UK. Before then, there had never been such widespread and mainstream opposition to North Sea oil and gas. This opposition is a direct result of decades of campaigning by so many people. Cambo was a tipping point. There was a huge amount of work that went into creating an environment for the success of a campaign like that to be possible.

But, you may be thinking, don't we need fossil-fuel companies for an energy transition to be possible?

These fossil-fuel companies have proven to us time and time again that they quite simply do not give a fuck about any of us. They don't care if we live or die. They don't care if we all go extinct. They don't care if our food systems collapse. They don't care if entire communities' only water supplies are poisoned. They don't care if they kill land defenders or wipe out entire communities. They care about one thing and one thing only: profit. We cannot trust them to act in our best interests. We cannot trust them to not continue to exploit. Exploitation is quite literally their business model. Remember that BP's original name was The First Exploitation Company.

Evidence reviewed by Amnesty International showed that Shell repeatedly encouraged the Nigerian military to deal with the community protests against its operations despite the horrific consequences that might follow.[59] Whilst working in Colombia, BP made payments – in the millions – to the Ministry of Defence, Colombian Army and others in order to 'protect' its oil facilities. Questions have been raised about the extent to which BP benefited from the human-rights abuses perpetrated by paramilitary groups along the pipeline.[60] In 2011, Chevron was found guilty in an Ecuadorian court and fined eight billion dollars for pollution that amounted to an ecological disaster and seriously harmed the human rights of the Indigenous inhabitants in a small and sensitive part of the rainforest.[61] Friends of The Earth France and Survie published an entire report titled 'A Nightmare Named Total' in 2020, which revealed the ongoing human-rights violations linked to Total's activities in Uganda and Tanzania, through projects including the East African Crude Oil Pipeline, which were impacting about 100,000 people.[62] All of these companies have also compromised workers' rights and opposed unions time and time again. That's only a few examples from a few companies. Just google 'human-rights abuses' along with the name of any fossil-fuel company and you'll find many, many more instances of violence.

If we want an energy system that protects both people and the planet, then we need to get as far away from these companies as possible and put our energy systems into public hands. We don't need private companies to control our energy. We shouldn't want them to. It should never be that the control over the provision and supply of something which is essential for the survival of people is put in the hands of a company driven by profit. It isn't hard to see that provision won't be given based on what's best for the people, but rather be driven by what is most profitable for the company.

This all being said, it's important that, rather than advocating for these industries to be shut down overnight, we call for a Just Transition. A Just Transition calls for a transition away from harmful fossil fuels to renewable energy that leaves no one behind; a transition that protects jobs and workers; a transition that can lead to enhanced workers' rights. The Climate Justice Alliance defines it as:

'A vision-led, unifying and place-based set of principles, processes, and practices that build economic and political power to shift from an extractive economy to a regenerative economy. This means approaching production and consumption cycles holistically and waste-free. The transition itself must be just and equitable; redressing past harms and creating new relationships of power for the future through reparations. If the process of transition is not just, the outcome will never be. Just Transition describes both where we are going and how we get there.'[63]

It is entirely possible that we have a transition to renewable energy that is still based upon the same extractivist ideals that the fossil-fuel industry has been using since its inception. Whilst we wouldn't be making the climate crisis worse in this future, it is still not climate justice. It is not the future we want. But it is the future we will get if we leave this transition to the fossil-fuel companies.

It's so important that we hold Just Transition principles close to us when we are advocating for climate justice. Often, a tactic used by the fossil-fuel industry or governments working against a liveable future is to say that climate campaigners are against workers or jobs. They say that we are advocating for shutting down the industry overnight, putting thousands of jobs and 'energy security' at risk. More recently, politician Kwasi Kwarteng, when Minister for the Department of Business, Energy and Industrial Strategy in the UK, weaponised the war in Ukraine to push this propaganda. After being challenged by activists on this, he tweeted:

'Shout and scream all you like, I'm not going to put Britain's energy security at risk by shutting off domestic oil and gas production. We need oil and gas for decades to come. Either we source more of what we need from the North Sea, or import more from abroad.'[64]

We have to make it clear that these statements are a misrepresentation of the truth – they're just oil and gas industry propaganda. We are calling for a Just Transition, not shutting down all fossil fuels overnight. The fossil-fuel industry is not on the side of their workers or the people. They consistently enact mass layoffs, create dangerous working environments and work to bust unions.

We have to keep workers' rights central to all of our climate organising. We have to listen to the very real worries that workers have in the face of these huge changes. We have to work with unions and workers together against our common enemy: the fossil-fuel industry, bosses and the capitalist system.

Kwarteng and the fossil-fuel industry not only weaponise workers and jobs, they also bring up the phrase 'energy security' a lot. They suggest that, by phasing out fossil fuels, we are putting that so-called 'security' at risk. In actual fact, fossil fuels are an energy source which is extremely wasteful, expensive and unreliable, whereas publicly owned renewable energy can increase energy autonomy and democracy, provide reliable energy supply (energy security) and reduce energy costs.[65] It takes energy provision out of the private hands that only exist for profit and puts it into the hands of the people. It is an essential demand of climate justice. We are seeing these projects spring up all over the world. In Bethesda in North Wales, Energy Local have worked with one hundred households to create an Energy Local Club with their local hydro plant.[66] This has allowed these residents – in an area with significant fuel poverty – to access cheaper energy directly from the local hydro plant, bypassing the big companies and the increased prices on the market. This project has made a real difference to these households.

So, what do we do about these fossil-fuel companies? What do we do about all of the exploitative companies?

As I write this, the UK government has just approved the Jackdaw gas field and the Abigail oil field in the North Sea and have created even more loopholes to promote oil and gas companies to extract even more. There are dozens more projects in the pipeline and we need to stop them all. It is important for us to understand that the fossil-fuel industry's days are numbered. They will not exist as fossil-fuel companies forever and will be forced to transition eventually. They know that too. Now, the question is not 'if' we stop them, but 'when'. Our role is to bring that 'when' far closer to the present so that we can save as many lives as possible, and to give us the best chance at preventing complete climate collapse.

There are a lot of things we can do.

We can and should always call out their greenwashing wherever we see it. You can join the brilliant Mary Annaise Heglar (@maryheglar), who is 'Greentrolling' them all on Twitter. We have a whole podcast episode about it on *The YIKES Podcast* if you're keen to understand it a bit more. We can talk more about the atrocities they have caused and make sure that everybody knows. We can divest our money from them by changing our banks and pensions to ones that don't have any investments in fossil fuels. If you're at university, check if your uni has divested yet, and if they haven't, join or start a campaign to make them! Most importantly, we can protest them at every opportunity. We can disrupt their AGMs, we can physically block them from carrying out fossil-fuel extraction, and we can protest every single time we see their presence in any space. We can make it so that they are unable to speak at any event, sponsor any exhibition, attend a conference, or even rent a space as the organisers will know that there would be far too much backlash if they allow it. Direct action is key here.

The fossil-fuel industry is undeniably one of the most powerful forces in the world. We have to meet that power with our own. We have to fight back. We have to fight back because a better future is so possible if we do. We can take them on when enough of us come together and are strategic about it. So, wherever you're at on your journey with all of this, join us in taking down the fossil-fuel industry brick by brick. I can already hear them starting to crumble.

6. TOO RADICAL OR NOT RADICAL ENOUGH?

'Radical simply means grasping things at the root.'

—Angela Y. Davis, feminist and civil-rights activist

'There has never been a major societal transformation in the history of mankind that has not been looked upon as unrealistic, idiotic, or utopian by the large majority of experts even a few years before the unthinkable became reality.'

—Sebastian Scheerer, sociologist

When hearing the phrase 'direct action', your immediate response might be that such acts are too radical. Or, in a different sense, when you first read the title of this book, you might have wondered if I was suggesting that being radical in our actions is a bad thing. The word 'radical' will have a different meaning for each one of us. Climate action itself will carry different meanings too. In order to build a better world, a multiplicity of actions are necessary, and therefore a multiplicity of roles are necessary too. Each role is valuable. Each role is important. Your role is important. There is often a misunderstanding that the only way to take action is to be the person in front of the microphone on the stage at a rally; someone on the streets protesting, or glueing yourself to the road. For people to even be able to carry out actions like these, there are so many people working behind the scenes filling out spreadsheets, sorting finances, writing out plans, doing outreach on the streets, researching to make information available, or facilitating meetings. There are people working from all kinds of different angles to apply pressure in other ways, in order to bring about change. My friend Tolmeia Gregory, who is a brilliant artist and illustrator who uses her talents to create change, often says that making a cup of tea for folks at meetings or actions is a vital role in the movement. If you've ever been put off from taking action because you thought it was all 'too radical', stay open to challenging that idea here, but also know that there *will* be a role for you in this movement, no matter what.

It's just after COP26 – the big UN Climate Change Conference hosted in Glasgow – and I'm preparing to go on *The Great Debate*, a Sky News show. This week's episode is all about COP26 and whether runaway climate change is inevitable. I'm texting a friend about how the panel isn't ideal. Two of the other panellists are Prime Minister Boris Johnson's COP26 spokesperson, Allegra Stratton, and

Australia's former Foreign Minister Alexander Downer; two people who are definitely not on the side of climate justice.

My friend texts me and says, 'Look, Mikaela, they will try to frame you as the radical. Double down on what you're saying as common sense.'

I am often framed as 'the radical' as a way to invalidate what I'm actually saying. In this context, 'radical' is seen as something irrational; something to be afraid of. Meanwhile, those who are promoting climate delay, upholding oppressive systems and enabling harm and devastation are simply seen as the norm.

Is the desire to create a safer, better world for all of us really that 'radical'? Isn't it something we should all want, not just for ourselves but for the generations that will come after us?

There is a never-ending debate going on in my head: *am I too radical or not radical enough?* This question follows me everywhere, and I don't think it will ever go away.

There have been so many times when I have been told I am 'too radical'. Whether it's for being vocally anti-capitalist, calling for the abolition of prisons and the police, risking arrest as part of direct action or taking the UK government to court in 2021, I have been chastised often for taking these actions. I've also been told – mostly on Twitter – that I'm not 'radical' enough. We'll get to that later.

But what does 'radical' really mean? Its true meaning is simply going to the root of an issue – to tackle it from where it came from. However, in the mainstream, it's often used as an insult, as if 'radical' is synonymous with 'absurd', 'ridiculous', 'destructive' or 'outrageous'. I think it's important here that we define all those things.

What is *outrageous* is the fact that we are currently on track globally for complete climate collapse because a very small percentage of people want to continue profiting from fossil fuels and overconsumption. What is *destructive* is the fact that entire nations will be submerged by human-caused rising sea levels in the coming years. What is *really absurd* is that we live in an economic system that allows for a few people to hoard more wealth than they could possibly spend in thousands of lifetimes, whilst so many do not have access to safe homes, food or water. And what is utterly *ridiculous* is that absolutely none of this is necessary; so much of it is preventable.

When addressing the world at a press conference for one of the most recent IPCC reports, UN Secretary-General António Guterres noted this irony:

'Climate activists are sometimes depicted as dangerous radicals. But the truly dangerous radicals are the countries that are increasing the production of fossil fuels. Investing in new fossil fuels infrastructure is moral and economic madness.'[67]

We really need to reframe what is and what is not ridiculous or outrageous. When we have been living in a system for so long, those calling for change are often painted as harmful, rather than those who work to continue the world as it currently is. Often, we can be scared to demand anything too far away from the current reality. We're scared of causing too much disruption or really rocking the boat. We stay with what is familiar because to go outside of that feels less comfortable to think about.

Sure, change is frightening. Moving away from what is already known to us is scary. But none of that is a good enough reason not to try and change the world for the better. None of that is a good enough reason not to take the necessary actions to prevent our extinction and an increase in suffering for billions along the way.

We also need to reframe what is possible. What is or is not radical is often based on what is currently believed to be within the realms of possibility. How is it that we already have so many solutions to the climate crisis that don't compromise human rights or justice, but the only solutions being seriously considered are the ones that do?

We have to remember that every single thing that governments or corporations do is a choice. It is a choice to continue to burn, fund and extract fossil fuels when there are alternative energy sources available. It is a choice to make 'net zero' targets that are dependent upon future technologies and dodgy carbon offsets rather than creating legislation which will actually get us to 'real zero' emissions. It is a choice to pay workers poverty wages, whilst bosses are making millions from their labour. When we remember that, and frame all of these things that impact our lives as choices, we can realise that other choices are entirely possible and should be demanded and made. So many of these choices are violent, but we have been made to normalise them. We have become so accustomed to this just being the way things are that we refuse to challenge, or even see, the societal violence around us.

Why is it that ending capitalism, whiteness and living in a world where all of us can live in dignity and safety can be harder to conceptualise than imagining the end of the world?

Imagination and having faith in a new world is the first step towards actually getting it. Allowing yourself the space to imagine and believe in the possibility of a new and better future does not have to mean that you are denying the realities of the world as it is now; it just means that you are not accepting that this has to be our fate. You are choosing to fight for a better one.

The world we are currently living in is the result of people's imaginations. We are walking around in the imaginations of others. Prisons are the result of someone's imagination. Capitalism is the result of certain people's imaginations. As we have discussed, racism and white supremacy are the result of someone's imagination – they have no scientific basis. But these imaginations have been so powerful that they have decimated cultures, justified mass kidnappings and genocides and are currently leading us towards our collective extinction. If imagining can be that powerful, we have to take hold of it ourselves. We have to prioritise it ourselves. We have to imagine – and believe in – our futures as much as those who created these systems believed in theirs.

When it comes to climate action, progress can be slow, and gained in small increments. As a result of this, it can be tempting to just accept whatever we do get as being better than nothing. The argument goes that green capitalism is better than just plain ol' capitalism; net zero is better than no agreements at all, and on and on it goes. I used to agree. Because if every single fraction of a degree that we can prevent matters, then to some extent, any action is helpful if it helps prevent that fraction of a degree. The thing is, I don't think we are helping to save degrees of warming or even fractions of degrees of warming by settling for less. The more we settle, the further we push back progress. The more that we accept weak offerings, the weaker our chances against runaway climate change gets. In her essay 'Bigger is Better in Medicine Stories: Essays for Radicals', Puerto Rican Jewish feminist writer Aurora Levins Morales frames it thus: 'when we can't yet have it all, we must choose the path that most expands our capacity to get it all in the future'.[68]

To understand this a bit more, let's talk about the Overton Window.

The Overton Window is a model for understanding how ideas within society change over time and influence politics. The window itself is representative of the existing political 'possibility': it's the range of ideas that the public deems reasonable and acceptable. It is dynamic and changes throughout time and place. It's connected to the 'social licence' idea that we explored in the previous chapter, but rather than being about a corporation, it's based on ideas and ideologies.

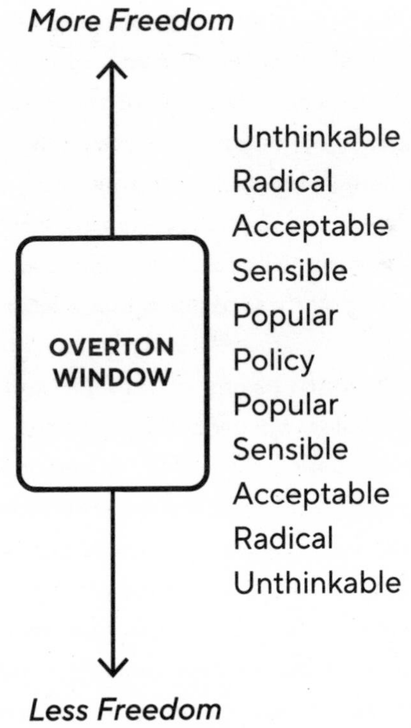

For example, from a UK perspective, ideas that previously would have been considered extreme or impossible, such as women having the right to vote, or queer couples being able to get married, are now widely viewed as common sense. That reflects a shift in the Overton Window.

It can work the other way around too, however. Many have said that the rise of politicians like Donald Trump and Boris Johnson also led to the Overton Window being shifted away from social progress in the Global North. By pushing violent anti-immigrant, racist rhetoric, both of these heads of state set the groundwork for building walls – real or figurative – to be normalised. We saw a horrendous result of this rhetoric when the UK government announced their plans to forcibly deport asylum seekers to Rwanda, where they would be processed and then unable to return to the UK. Whilst this plan still seems – and is still – completely abhorrent to many, the fact that this was implemented and popular with the British public shows that a shift has occurred. For this policy to be seen as acceptable, despite going against international law and involving human beings being forcibly taken and detained in a country far away after already having journeyed so far to find safety and family, shows the power of shifting the Overton Window in just a short space of time.

On a more positive note, we can also use the power of shifting the window for good. That requires us to demand more, rather than less.

The current position of the Overton Window makes all of the awful things that continue to worsen the climate crisis to be perceived as 'normal' or 'acceptable'. The fact that the window currently sits in this place at all is due to the oligarch-run mainstream media; fossil-fuel lobbying groups; the billionaires; the big corporations – all those who hold power and wish to maintain that power. As much as we can wish it, their power won't just simply go away. It will still be a force that scrambles to pull the window further to a place that benefits them completely. I think it can be helpful to imagine this as a sort of tug of war over ideas. If you'll forgive the pretty questionable metaphor (I'm sure it has limitations), by viewing it in this way, we can visualise all those who profit from climate destruction and exploitation pulling from one side and the majority of us who want a liveable, safe future on the other side. If the power on each side is equal, then the window would sit somewhere in the middle of both of these ideas. For this metaphor, the distance pulled from each side is dependent on two things: the power they hold and how far along the spectrum their ideas sit. We can tackle their power using all the tactics we have discussed thus far, but it's also important for us to be offering a genuinely radical, transformative alternative. We have to demand what we really want and need. We have to imagine and demand the most transformative 'radical' ideas – knowing we might not get those met any time soon – so that what we do achieve is as close to it as is actually possible. If we settle for less in what we are demanding, then our ideas just get toned down even more and the result is pulled even further away from what is actually needed.

Already, the climate movement, along with other social movements, has managed to pull this window a bit further towards what is needed on so many fronts. Whether it's the movement of language away from 'climate change' to 'climate crisis/emergency' or the fact that any climate policy even exists and is so popular – this is all the result of huge amounts of campaigning to make ideas that were originally considered to be 'niche' or 'fringe' to now become mainstream.

But some NGOs toning down our demands have also delayed our progress. Whether it's calling for green capitalism rather than anti-capitalism, refusing to challenge growth narratives or sacrificing racial justice in their messaging; in trying to be pragmatic, the future we need has been getting further and further from us.

I'm not against pragmatism or small wins. I think that it's important in some ways and in certain spaces. But it's often misused. Rather than being pragmatic in a tactical sense, in pursuit of liberation, pragmatism is often used to give up on a liberated world and force us to settle for less.

Often the compromise in settling are lives and livelihoods in the Global South. Whether it's the Western-centric Green New Deal, or relying on new 'green' technologies, the sacrifice or compromise being made here is of entire cultures, communities, homelands and peoples in the Global South. We absolutely cannot allow that.

Over the years, I've had to learn to be more practical in how I communicate about this crisis. I've had to remind myself that, in building the power we need to actually create – and not just talk about creating – a climate-just future, it is necessary for us to reach a lot of people. It requires us to not only rely on knowledge or awareness as having the power to change the world, but really, practically working out how we can organise people to take action. It's that switch that can be difficult, but that move is exactly what we need. Decades of climate work based on the principle that 'if only people knew then they would act' has shown us that that approach is simply not enough. Knowledge of an impending crisis is not enough. Even experiencing a crisis is often not enough. What *is* enough is a programme that actually offers material improvements to the lives of people today. This is what is really needed if we are going to win this fight.

In being practical, I've taken actions within our current system. One of those actions was taking the UK government to court in 2021. Whilst to some, this would be seen as a 'radical' action to have taken, for others in movement spaces it's been seen as the opposite. I've been criticised for choosing to be a claimant in that case. Some have observed that, because my actions in going through the courts work within the system rather than outside of it, it could be strengthening and validating our legal system. It could be suggesting that true justice always comes from the courts. I can understand these criticisms. I can appreciate them. I also agree with aspects of them. To be honest, I found the court case a very difficult action to be a part of.

In the past, I had been clear to myself about wanting to work outside the system, not within it. Two years before I put my name on the Paid To Pollute court case, I'd chained myself to a metal tube in the middle of the road in Westminster, right outside the Department for Business, Energy and Industrial Strategy, making myselfvulnerable to arrest.

I had spent that week in October 2019 occupying the roads around the department, right outside Westminster Abbey, with Extinction Rebellion Scotland. Our occupation site was called 'Power In Truth' and was there to bring the public's attention to the huge fossil-fuel subsidies and tax breaks the government allows the industry. We camped on the road in our tents, spent all day running workshops, hosting speeches and music on our stage, sharing food, creating social-media content, bringing about actions against the department, carrying out interviews and more.

It was on the third day of our occupation that the police

closed in on us, seizing unmanned tents, removing our infrastructure and arresting those who got in the way. What had been a hopeful site was now only being held by a dozen people, glued or chained to different pieces of our infrastructure in the hope that this would maintain our occupation. Police surrounded us, warning us that by staying we were making ourselves liable to arrest. I wondered how I'd ended up as one of these people.

At the time, this was the most 'radical' thing I'd been involved with. Having read Dr Martin Luther King Junior's *Letter From a Birmingham Jail*, and having learned about the importance of direct action in pushing progress in civil rights movements all over the world, my hesitancy was not a result of me thinking that this tactic was unimportant or too much. For me, as a medical student, my reluctance came from not wanting to compromise my future career with a criminal record.[‡‡‡‡] I was in my third year of medical studies and getting in wasn't easy for me. I had worked myself into the ground at school and, despite always achieving perfect grades in exams, I was frequently predicted lower ones by teachers – something which happens often to Black students – and this had impacted me getting a place at medical school the first time around. Up until this point in my life, nothing had felt more important to me than becoming a doctor. Still greater than my concerns around having a criminal record was my fear of the police. I understood that, as someone racialised as Black, interactions with the police were more

‡‡‡‡ I later found out that arrests for peaceful protests don't necessarily compromise your fitness to practise as a doctor. I'm just adding this in for any other medics so you don't get scared off from taking part in direct action. Check out groups like Doctors for XR and MedAct for more up-to-date info on this.

dangerous for me than for my white comrades.

Earlier that day, I'd taken part in a live reading of the 1.5 degrees IPCC report – written by the world's leading climate scientists – after which I had broken down and cried. The section I read was about the effect of 1.5 degrees of warming on coral reefs, marine ecosystems and coastal communities. It was as if, in that moment, I was able to feel the weight of all the things we had been talking about over the last few days. It suddenly hit my heart, and it broke. All the information I'd known in my head became more than just facts, more than far-away ideas; I'd broken down whatever barrier I'd been holding up to stop me from feeling the severity of this. I'd known that the climate crisis was causing forced migration, droughts, loss of species and ecosystem collapse, but I hadn't really allowed myself to feel it. Once I did, it hit me like a wave.

So, when I was asked whether I would 'lock-on' – a process in which an activist glues, chains or attaches themself by other means to some sort of infrastructure in order to make it much harder for the police to remove them – to help prevent the police from taking our site, I said yes. I spent an emotional eight hours locked to our stage[§§§§] in a police cordon until the middle of the night, when they let us walk free if we unlocked ourselves then and there.[*****]

I risked arrest because I truly believed we had no other options left to us. I'd done all the things we are told to do. I

---

§§§§ You can find a video of me locked-on, speaking about why I made that decision, on my Instagram page, @mikaelaloach – you'll have to scroll down a bit to find it.

***** I think it's important to add here that whilst a bunch of us did unlock and walk in that moment, two brave people decided to stay. John, 67, who had been locked in the same arm tube as me, was one of the two who stayed. They were arrested at 4.30 a.m.

believed there was nothing else I could do to help other than put my liberty on the line. Direct action is truly a last resort. I believe that, when used strategically, direct action really works. It gets the goods. And that's why the UK government is currently trying to prevent all forms of it.

During this time, I firmly believed that doing anything within the system – that is, through court cases, formal political parties and so on – was a complete waste of time, and that the only way we could create real change was to put the pressure on and cause disruption from the outside.

Whilst I still deeply believe that direct action is an essential tactic in the fight for climate justice and a liveable planet, and that for so many, there is no option but to do it in order to survive, I now know that it is not the *only* way to create change. I see the pitfalls in prescribing a single solution for a crisis this huge. I also now recognise the dangers around glorifying arrest and using it as a goal, rather than a necessary consequence of our actions. As with anything we do, we need to ask ourselves questions about why we are taking a certain action, and ensure that those actions are strategic.

My understanding of the famous quote from Audre Lorde's essay 'The Master's Tools Will Never Dismantle the Master's House' informed my opinion that the only way we can create real change is from outside of the system. From this, I had completely rejected any idea of using existing institutions or structures to create justice. I still question it. I wonder if, by using current institutions and manipulating or reforming them to work for our cause, we are simply allowing these structures to adapt and continue to exist.

However, when reading the essay itself, I came to realise that Lorde was not saying that we cannot ever successfully use the system to create revolutionary change. She was instead saying that we must not replicate the same structures that have created oppression in the way we are fighting for change. She was commenting on the lack of intersectionality; the lack of inclusion of perspectives from the most marginalised in the work that was being done in the name of revolutionary change, particularly by white feminists. Lorde was writing about the need to not replace systems of patriarchy, oppression and individualism in our activist work, but the need instead to build community, coalition, connection and an appreciation for our shared and different struggles. Here, the 'Master's Tools' that Lorde refers to are those of separation and division. She writes: 'In our world, divide and conquer must become define and empower.'

The full context of Lorde's famous quote is as follows:

'Those of us who stand outside the circle of this society's definition of acceptable women; those of us who have been forged in the crucibles of difference – those of us who are poor, who are lesbians, who are Black, who are older – know that survival is not an academic skill. It is learning how to take our differences and make them strengths. For the master's tools will never dismantle the master's house. They may allow us temporarily to beat him at his own game, but they will never enable us to bring about genuine change. And this fact is only threatening to those women who still define the master's house as their only source of support.'[69]

Ahead of partaking in any action, I ask myself the following questions:

- Does this have the potential to create lasting change?
- How does this fit onto our roadmap for a completely transformed and liberated world?
- Will this help to shift the Overton Window closer to a place that allows us a liveable future?

- Will this help improve the material conditions of the lives of those most affected and oppressed?
- Could this prevent any of the above?
- Is this just a distraction from work that could truly build a new world?
- What can I do to modify or change this action so that it cannot be co-opted?
- With arrestable actions, it's also important to add: is it essential for this to be arrestable?

Whilst our court case against the UK government was far from perfect, I kept those questions in mind throughout the process. I also kept the raging, twenty-one-year-old version of myself who locked her arm into that tube alongside me, challenging me at every step of the way. In doing so, we focused on creating a campaign and legacy around the case itself. In our communications, we made it clear that justice is not only won in the courts, but also on the streets. The success of this case in moving us forward would not be solely dependent on the decision of a judge.

We put the effort in to build a concerted media campaign around the case so that even if we lost in court, which we sadly did, then we would have raised awareness of the fact that the UK government has paid – and continues to pay – billions of pounds of public money to North Sea oil and gas companies every single year. We managed to get the oil and gas subsidies, which prop up the industry but rarely get any focus, back onto the agenda. We also managed to get the UK government to admit to the fact that they were giving oil and gas companies huge tax breaks and subsidies.

This case was just one of many tactics. Others all over the world have used the legal system to try to get us towards climate justice. In the same year as our case, a group of activists in the Netherlands won a successful case against fossil-fuel giant Shell; in Ecuador, Indigenous Peoples won a historic climate case against their government in 2022; and the UK government has lost multiple court battles with green groups over their shameful net-zero strategy, their funding of fossil fuel-projects in Mozambique and many other issues. The success of all these campaigns comes about because the legal cases are *only one part* of the tactics used. Whilst I don't believe that the legal system will get us the true justice we need, I do now believe that we can use parts of the system – not just the legal system – to move towards climate justice if we are strategic and critical about it and, perhaps most importantly, don't let the system tell us what is and what is not possible.

Often, if someone is telling you that something isn't radical enough, then there is probably something of value that you can take from that. Our imaginations will be clouded, shaped and restricted by the current systems, which will limit how far we are able to imagine and what is believed to be possible. Challenging each other and untangling our imaginations and perspectives from the status quo is part of this necessary work. I think that we can – and should – push the limits of the possible and learn from those who are forced to take seemingly radical actions every single day, simply in order to survive in the face of extractivists.

We must also learn from the abolitionists movements that have made the impossible possible over and over again. When you hear about abolition, your mind might first go to ideas of policing or prisons. In 2020, with the resurgence of the Black Lives Matter movement, the conversation around prison and police abolition came to the fore once again. Many who did not understand abolition saw it as a demand for all policing to end overnight, and for prisons to be immediately emptied. This scare tactic of misconstruing the meaning of abolition is also used by governments, who claim that climate activists are calling for the fossil-fuel industry to be shut down overnight, putting thousands of jobs and our energy supply at risk. In both cases, this understanding of abolition is wrong.

Abolition is a process. Angela Davis encapsulates it perfectly in the title of her first book on the topic: *Are Prisons Obsolete?* Abolition is not about shutting these harmful institutions down overnight. Rather, it's about transforming the world so that these institutions – policing, prisons and the fossil-fuel industry – become obsolete. Abolition is about love and care. It's not only about phasing out and taking down the institutions that cause harm and incite violence, but it's also about building a new and better world; a world in which we tackle the things that force people into crime: poverty, insecurity, the patriarchy, and more, rather than just resorting to state violence and incarceration to 'solve' the problem.

What people refer to in this debate as 'reform', on the other hand, are actions that hope to mould the existing system to be better. Green capitalism is a 'green' reform of capitalism, for example. This might seem like a good idea in theory, given that it suggests an improvement on the existing system, but in actual fact reform often allows a harmful system to exist for longer. It enables it to adapt, evolve and survive. Rather than wanting a harmful system to cause less harm, shouldn't we want a new system altogether? Don't we deserve that?

So how do we find the parts of the system that we can use whilst not playing into reform and allowing harmful systems to adapt, evolve and survive for longer? When working out all of these questions, like so many other questions I had whilst writing this book, I spoke to some friends about it all. In these conversations, Rhiannon Osborne, a fellow medical student, close friend and all-round totally wonderful human, introduced me to the concept of non-reformist reform.

'Non-reformist reform' is a term coined by Austrian–French theorist André Gorz that challenges the binary debate between abolition, revolution and reform as tactics for ushering in a liberated and transformed world. Unlike the pragmatism or reform that maintains the existing status quo, non-reformist reform refers to the gradual and more immediate wins that must be made on the path to a fully transformed and liberated society. Gorz states that 'a non-reformist reform is determined not in terms of what can be, but what should be.'[70]

The fight for better pay and conditions for workers by unions could be classified as non-reformist reform. Whilst the results of this action don't achieve everything necessary for a complete transformation – the power and control of production remains in the hands of bosses rather than workers – it nevertheless achieves a necessary win on the way to complete transformation. It disrupts power dynamics while also improving the current lives of oppressed people, thereby creating the conditions for the oppressed to better organise and continue to push for liberation. It also keeps the longer-term, bigger picture in mind.

Whilst not referring to what she writes about as explicitly non-reformist reform, Aurora Levins Morales goes into these ideas in her essay 'Bigger Is Better':

'When we think big, hope is no longer deferred. Our small steps add up to a journey. We stop thinking that limiting our scope increases our chances. We don't throw anyone overboard for the sake of a little gain. When we think big, we fight for everyone.'[71]

As we've discussed, existential threats are nothing new. The necessity to believe in and act on a radical imagination of the future is not new. My ancestors, who were kidnapped from their Indigenous lands on the African continent, chained, shoved into boats destined for the Caribbean and forced to labour day and night, had to believe that this fate was not sealed. They had to believe that the world could be radically transformed. Not only did they have to believe it, they had to act with this belief. They took drastic action, not because they knew they would win but because making the world safe and better is always worth it. There is simply no other way to radically transform the world than to believe in it and do it.

Everything can change. Every single thing. Nothing is immutable. Once you know that – once you believe that everything can change and that everything that has been changed matters – that's when we can transform the world around us. We have always had that power; it simply requires us to recognise it.

So much of our action and success hinges on storytelling and on rewriting the narrative we have been told. Some of it depends on redefining language, some of it on being willing to let language go when it's no longer working. But to change this story, all of us need to start telling a new one. We need to push that Overton Window over.

How can our actions be both radical – in the true meaning of the word, by going to the root of the problem and creating a new world – whilst also being mindful of the need to create a politics that wins? Or, to put it another way, how can our actions be inherently radical whilst still strategically appealing to the vast swathes of people that are required for revolutionary change to be possible?

I think that a huge part of this requires us to look at the

language we are using. Is the use of certain terminology more of a help or a hindrance in a particular situation? Could we instead say what we really mean? Depending on the context, could we say 'obsolescence' instead of 'abolition'? Could we say 'goes to the root' in place of 'radical'? I think that the importance here is that what we really mean isn't being sacrificed. We aren't actually toning down our demands. We aren't making them conform to the system. We are just finding a way to communicate our demands so that they will be listened to and understood. I think that, in the contexts we are facing, this sort of practicality is of the utmost importance.

The work we are doing should be able to create a new world. It should be about improving the material conditions of those who are most oppressed in society. It should be about protecting all of us from complete planetary destruction. It should not simply be about ticking boxes by saying those things that the people who already care and are already taking action want us to say. It needs to be about transformation.

I want us to win. But I want us to win a future worth fighting for. That means a future free from white supremacy, capitalist exploitation and all other forms of oppression. For us to win this future, it requires us to fight back strategically and to communicate effectively.

A vital part of this conversation is the fact that many people believe that unless they can and are willing to do the 'most radical' actions in pursuit of liberation – that is, in a UK context, risk arrest – then they shouldn't do anything at all. That is untrue. We really do need everyone to do whatever they can, wherever they can, however they can. We really need a multiplicity of tactics.

As I've discussed, and will go on to explore more in the next chapter, I definitely haven't always held radical political views or carried out radical actions. The first action I ever took that had any intention of helping the wider world was to organise a bake sale at my school in support of victims of a tsunami when I was five years old. Taking that small action was the first thing that showed me that we do not have to be passive in the face of injustice, and that, when we are organised and work with others, the change we create can be so much bigger. From there, as I grew older, I did the things we are told to do: the lifestyle changes, the fundraising and awareness-raising activities. I volunteered with local organisations during my summer holidays. None of this was going-to-the-roots-of-the-issue stuff, but it was still important work. Each of these actions taught me more about the different ways we can create change; how to organise with people to build something bigger than that which came before, and a greater understanding of the multiplicity of struggles in this world. When I began working on climate activism, so much of what I was doing was still centred on individualistic lifestyle changes as the goal, and I was still focused on simply raising awareness, but I was nevertheless learning and growing a lot in my politics and communication skills. Similarly, when it came to racism, I was, for a time, stuck on tackling or calling out interpersonal racism rather than going to the roots of white supremacy, but I was nevertheless constantly growing in my understanding of whiteness. It's true that the actions I carried out didn't threaten or fundamentally challenge the pillars of various oppressive systems, because I didn't yet know how, but they were still vital steps on the path that led me to where I am today. Now I can see that I was acting to tackle the symptoms of those systems rather than addressing the systems themselves, and upon reflection, there are a variety of reasons why I didn't go beyond those types of actions; reasons that may be familiar to many of us.

For one thing, I genuinely thought that these actions alone were enough. I gravely misunderstood the bigger picture. I also didn't believe that it was possible to fundamentally change the systems that the world is built upon. I didn't realise that another way was possible.

Next, I didn't understand the power of things like direct action and community organising, and finally, if I'm really honest, I didn't think things were 'bad enough' to require more radical responses. This perspective came from a huge amount of privilege.

Learning about and understanding how social movements have won ground in the past, and seeing more and more movements taking on tactics of direct action all over the world, challenged my hesitation and changed my mind. The 2018 IPCC report, combined with the rise of the Movement for Black Lives and increased awareness of widespread oppression globally, transformed my perspective completely on my final belief that things weren't bad enough to justify taking more radical action. All of this – my renewed understanding of the multiplicity of crises we face, the severity of the climate crisis, and the willingness to try to tackle it that I had been building since I was five, came together. I joined Extinction Rebellion Scotland and put myself in several situations where I stood to be arrested. All of these steps have ultimately led me to all of the organising work I've done to this day. Being in London during the October Rebellion brought me a huge amount of hope and truly redirected my life, but I would never have made it to that point or any of the work I do now if I had not had the experiences that came before.

I'm sharing my journey to demonstrate the fact that no action is too small. We have no way of knowing where it might lead. That bake sale when I was five years old paved the way for me to participate in non-violent direct action and take the UK government to court. I didn't grow up in an activist household or with friends doing this sort of work, so I had to learn along the way. I might have taken a bit longer than others, but that doesn't matter. Along that whole journey, I was gradually understanding more and moving closer towards getting it right. That's the way I view this work. It's not about getting it all right the first time. In fact, it's about realising that there simply isn't one 'right' way of doing it. It's about constantly challenging ourselves to understand more, and pushing ourselves to take the actions that will be the most strategic in actually getting to the root of these oppressive systems.

So, wherever you are on this journey, do what you can and push yourself a bit beyond that every single time. Don't just sit in what's comfortable, for being comfortable has never transformed the world. The world has always been changed by people choosing to be brave. People choosing to take one step further. What is brave for me might look very different to what's brave for you. But, in the face of lives being consumed by oppression and a climate crisis decimating the world, all I am asking of you is to be brave.

If you are someone who has been told they are 'too much' or 'too radical' for wanting a world where we are all safe and loved, remember that that desire – for dignity, for safety and for everyone to be OK – comes from the softest part of your soul. To be moved to take an action that builds something better from the horrors of this world is the most human thing you can do. It is the reasonable response. Hold onto your soft heart. Remember the love that pushes you forward and don't let go of it.

7. YOU DON'T KNOW WHAT YOU DON'T KNOW

'I have a vision of movement as a sanctuary. Not a tiny perfectionist utopia behind miles of barbed wire and walls and fences and tests and judgments and righteousness, but a vast sanctuary where our experiences, as humans who have experienced and caused harm, are met with centered, grounded invitations to grow.'

—adrienne maree brown, We Will Not Cancel Us

I was eighteen years old and at the start of a gap year, as I'd been rejected from every medical school I'd applied to. I spent my weekends visiting friends at their various universities to pass the time and find some joy whilst I worked various temp jobs during the weeks. This time, I was back in Edinburgh, the city where I would move the following year for my medical degree. I'd already come here once to visit friends and get over a break-up, and during that time I had met a few people. We were drinking in the common room of their halls when I saw a familiar face from the last time I had been there – a guy who I'd stayed up all night with chatting about communism when I got locked out of my friends' room.

'Hi,' I smiled. As he stumbled closer, I came to realise that he had probably had too much to drink already. 'You're so liberal,' he spat, with what I can only describe as complete disgust in his eyes. Eighteen-year-old Mikaela asked him to explain what he meant by that, to which he just repeated himself with the same manner and walked off. After our meeting, I assumed that he had found my teenage blog, read it, and was less than impressed with what he saw.

Six years on, I'm telling this anecdote because I think it's pretty exemplary of how so many of us interact with each other. We see what someone has written or said and we label them as having a certain political standpoint, or being a specific type of person morally, and denounce them for it rather than attempting to engage in change. If someone isn't at the exact place that we are now, we either look down on them or oust them altogether. It's pretty ironic that those of us who profess to want a more equitable world behave in this way, because it is not only counterproductive but all too often rooted in classism. That man in Edinburgh's disdain for me wasn't based on that, but it remains pertinent when considering how we respond to folks who are new to movements and who might slip up or not understand all the lingo. Not everyone has had the same access to education, resources or environment, and these are all key things that inform our politics.

The better world we are aiming for is contingent on a bunch of people who currently hold certain beliefs or ideas of the world, many of which come from their own lived experiences, changing their minds and being transformed. We need to see change from a lot of people who currently behave in ways that uphold oppressive systems and proliferate the climate crisis. In order for this to happen, space needs to be made for transformation, and for people to be allowed the dignity of their own journeys and to find their own way. A new world is utterly reliant on us being able to see the humanity in all people, even if those people can't see *our* humanity. It's a hard pill to swallow.

Rather than completely rejecting people for not holding the same political beliefs or being in the same place on their journey, it's vital that we hold space to understand why they believe what they do, and share the reasoning behind our own beliefs. We will get a lot further in this work if we approach each other from a place of seeing each other's shared humanity, rather than falling into binaries of good and bad.

For me to get to the place I am now, I had to go on a journey. When I was eighteen, I was still learning. I didn't fully understand how change happens and I would encourage fairly weak tactics. But all of that was part of my journey into understanding more. If I had been a different person, or if I had let that encounter in Edinburgh get into my head a bit more, then maybe I would have been pushed off my path due to the rejection. Sadly, this happens to all too many people. They begin to care and learn things, and then they get something wrong and feel rejected by the people who are now their peers. That rejection can push people away rather than bringing them closer to our understanding.

We have to move beyond the narrative that you can't do anything about a particular issue because you don't know enough, or the idea that 'smarter people' than you have it covered. The idea that you don't know enough to tackle the climate crisis, to demand better, to do the work to transform our world, only benefits the fossil-fuel industry, the big bosses and elites who do not want the world to fundamentally change. That narrative serves them. I assure you that we not only need you to resist this internal narrative so you can take up some of the work, but also that you have so much unique knowledge from your own life that will be vital in building a climate-just future.

If a lot of what you've read in this book so far has been new information to you, then that is completely OK. None of us leap from the womb as perfectly formed and unproblematic people who know all there is to know. It's brave to challenge yourself and open yourself to new possibilities and ideas of the world, and I'm really fucking proud of you for doing it.

There is a tendency to place every person in a box labelled 'good' or 'bad'. If they say obviously racist things, then they are 'bad'. If they organise in their local climate group, they're 'good'. But, of course, the world is never that simple.

This binary plays out at an absolute level, so that we often view others as completely, inherently good or completely, inherently bad. We ourselves don't want to be on the bad side, so those whose ideas about the world that differ from our own must be wholly bad.

This is just untrue. We are all a mix of good and bad and everything in between. Humans are messy and nuanced. We make choices and we get things wrong. What is brilliant is that we all have the capacity to change the choices we make. We do not have to follow one singular path, and yet the good or bad binary says otherwise.

This binary presents itself in many different ways, but it is most prevalent when we talk about historical figures. Those people who played key roles in changing the world are often presented to us as either entirely good and perfect, or completely bad and awful. The discussion around the British prime minister Winston Churchill is a key example of this. In UK history classes and the mainstream media, Churchill is presented to the public as a hero: a man who won the war against Nazism. He is presented as 'good'. But, whilst he did take many important actions to end the Second World War and save many European lives, he was also undeniably racist.

'Keep England White' was floated by Churchill as a campaign slogan for the 1955 election.[72] As part of his strategy during the war, he deliberately enacted policies that resulted in the 1943 Bengal famine, starving almost three million people in India. This was not just an accidental consequence, but a result of the lack of value he had for the lives of the people who were killed by the famine. Due to this, and many other racist actions by Churchill, many have called for this information to be taught alongside his successes, and for statues of the former prime minister to be taken down. In response, others have felt that highlighting these atrocities automatically places Churchill in the 'bad' category, and therefore, rather than acknowledging the harms he has caused, they have acted in defence of him.

A lot of this backlash against representing someone's full history wholly and honestly comes from the fact that we find it very difficult to see that people are multifaceted and nuanced, rather than objectively good or bad. If we accept and acknowledge this multiplicity, then we have to come to terms with and start working through the bad parts of ourselves: our own biases and the harm we might be causing. I'm not suggesting that all of us might unknowingly be causing a literal famine like Churchill did, but given the interconnectedness of all of our actions, we might be enabling others to do so.

It's vital for us to contend with the mixed-up reality of ourselves, so that we don't run the risk of continually perpetuating harm. Speaking on this phenomenon in an Instagram video, educator Rynnstar (@therealrynnstar) says: 'If you can never see yourself in the bad guys, you can never identify the biases in your own life . . . If you think you could never be the villain, you might be one.'[73]

This good and bad binary often results in folks believing that if someone is put in the 'bad' category, they must be banished or erased from society. When this happens, that person is completely dehumanised.

This is exactly what prisons do: rather than acting to understand or prevent harm, we hide those we have deemed to have caused harm in faraway cages. Prisons work on the basis that the harms caused in the world are just the result of a few 'bad apples', and that removing those people will reduce harm. Despite significant evidence showing that increased incarceration levels and prison populations does not lead to a reduction in crime, this logic is still widely believed to be true.††††† What *does* bring about a decrease in crime is tackling the things that lead people to it in the first place: poverty, oppression, exclusion at school, poor social care and so on.

What might it look like if, rather than simply pushing away the bad parts or ignoring their existence, we actually grappled with them? What if we tried to work out how they came to be, how they were or are upheld, and then worked out how to prevent them from happening again? How much prison systems have invaded our minds and how we interact with each other?

As a student doctor, I've had to look beyond the binaries of good and bad. Through my placements on hospital wards or GP surgeries, I have been forced to go beyond my climate-activist echo-chambers and find myself face to face with so many different people with different views and different lives. In healthcare environments, patients will often be incredibly vulnerable and honest with you – in that dynamic, people will often tell you what they think, whether you ask them to or not. It's an inherent level of trust that people place in medical professionals, and it isn't something I take lightly. No matter who my patient is, I am forced every single time to see the person I'm treating in the fullness of their humanity in order to treat them best, whether they can see mine or not. In those situations, it's often easier to see that fullness; often, in illness, our humanity is laid bare. We see a person for more than their worst parts and it's such a

††††† Prison logic also dictates that 'punishment' and threats of it will cause someone to change. We'll get into that later on. If you are interested in learning more about prison abolition work in the UK, I highly recommend reading *Brick By Brick: How We Build A World Without Prisons* by Cradle Community.

deep honour that we are offered that glimpse. But I try not to limit this to my medical career. I actively choose to see no stranger everywhere I go.

Choosing to see no stranger transformed my life. The concept states that we must view every single human as our kin, our family, as someone we love. We are all human, and all connected in some way, and therefore none of us are truly strangers. To see no stranger is to open one's heart to empathy; to try and see every person as a nuanced, messy person. When I am in a situation with someone where empathy is required, rather than distancing myself from this person, I pause. I think, *who do I love that I can see in this person? What is there that could be unknown to me about this person that would make me love them?* Sometimes I can see something of myself, a trace of a close friend, echoes of my dad, mum, brother or grandma. I can always see a piece of someone.

It has helped to not harden myself to the world completely yet. I think soft hearts are so important. We need soft hearts that will break and move us into action. We need soft hearts that will love all of us so deeply that the world will be changed for the better. I really believe that this constant reminder of the humanity – and complexity – of every single one of us has made my outlook on the world and communication so much better. To lean into our shared humanity opens all of us up to a greater possibility of being transformed and thus transforming the world around us.

Often, we forget that what people do is make choices. This extends to governments themselves, given that they are simply made up of people. Human beings are not in a default position or 'mode'. They make choices and they can and will make a variety of them, which means that they *can* change. This also means that we ourselves can change.

The good or bad binary doesn't just get in our way of seeing the reality of the world; it also has an impact on allowing power to go unquestioned and for those without power to be dehumanised and made into characters that are only capable of acting in a certain way. When we define someone as fully evil, we remove their humanity. They become separate from us – unable to be understood.

This binary happens because a simplification of the world is easier for our brains – we want to choose the path of least resistance. We don't want to have to challenge our own biases and therefore we assume that those who have them are significantly different and far away from our own humanity. Whilst this can happen to people in power, it can also be used by the ruling classes to dehumanise those on the margins of society.

This simplification also occurs because it benefits those who have power to retain it. Simplification of the world stops us from challenging the reasons why those who hold power have it. It stops people from challenging anything.

Although it can seem difficult, we *must* lean into the many complexities in this world.

Binaries are often arbitrary and ridiculous; in all of our many ways, we are all on a spectrum. As humans, we are complex, messy beings with an astounding ability to change and grow. Rather than being afraid of that, we must lean into it. We must challenge these binaries as often as we can.

This is one of the many reasons that I believe that transness is so hopeful for us all. The fact that people are coming out and resisting the gender binary, showing that there are a thousand different ways to be a person highlights the arbitrary nature of binaries. Even more than that – many of the 'rules' or 'systems' that we are force-fed by society are arbitrary too. Non-binary artist Jacob V. Joyce puts it perfectly:

'The existence of trans people presents a threat to one of the central tenets of the white-supremacist, capitalist state – that we all need to just accept our place within its violent system.'[74]

Writer and educator Fopé Ajanaku expands on this idea by saying that drawing attention to the cruelty of the gender binary would cause people to question:

'What else underpins the mechanisms of oppression in the world? They would begin to ask, "How does capital work? How does money work? How does race work? How does class work?" Once you unpick it, you have to unpick everything. The question then is, what's at stake? What's the cost here? And the conclusion is that the cost is too high, so they're more willing to police gender identity than to deal with anything else.'[75]

I want you to take a moment and try to think back to how you saw the world when you were a young kid. Back then, I doubt you knew much about oppressive systems, capitalism or any of the rules that dictate our world. Back then, it's possible that you believed lots of these rules didn't make any sense. *Why are people hungry when we have so much food getting thrown away in supermarkets all over the world? Why are people left unhoused when there are thousands of houses sitting empty? Why does money dictate who lives and dies when it's just a bunch of paper and metal?*

I remember wondering all of these things as a kid. I remember challenging all of these things and asking 'why' constantly. This outlook that young people have is often called naivety. These ideas or questions are dismissed because of the lack of experience a child has with the world. What others may call naivety in youth, I see as something deeply valuable and sacred, something essential that may get lost elsewhere. The refusal to accept that the world as it is now is as good as it gets is what pushes the world ever closer towards justice. Young people choose to imagine a world that is as free, radical and wonderful as possible. That is our default. That is what we are made to feel deep in our souls. It just gets ground out of us.

In a conversation on the *New Constellations* podcast, Farzana Khan, co-founder and executive director of Healing Justice London, speaks beautifully on the importance of young people in Islam:

'The child is the soul that just came into the body and the elder is returning. They're the closest to truth because they're not in the facades of social constructs. So, there's also so much wisdom in the soul of the child, and truth.'[76]

As a child, we were also used to being wrong a lot because we were aware that we don't and can't know it all – we learn as we live and grow. We don't have the same fragility as adults do about getting things wrong because we are allowed to still be moulded by the world and our experience. I think there is so much that we can learn from kids about this, and from the way in which we allow space for young people to get things wrong and learn – perhaps, we should hold onto a lot of that for adults too.

Of course, this all leads us to perfectionism. Binaries – moral or gender ones – are linked to white supremacy and capitalism. Under these systems, our worth is based on being better than someone else: being more productive, having more money, more power, being at greater proximity to 'whiteness'. We are told that unless we are at or near the top of these factors, we are worthless. Unless we are perfect and make no mistakes, we are worthless. So we pursue perfectionism. In the climate world, this is even more prevalent. Despite knowledge of how systems around us work and the logic that this stance is counterproductive to our aims, we can still suggest that unless you live a perfectly eco-friendly life, you can't say or do anything about the climate crisis. We pursue an unattainable goal because we are scared that if we don't, we will have no value at all. This inevitably leads us to react to criticism with fragility. We stick to what we know and rarely challenge ourselves because of this fear: because we have made our worth contingent on the success markers of these systems.

Jess Mally, anti-racism educator, writer and consultant, suggests a way out of this fragility with her Healthy Humans framework. In a conversation for *The YIKES Podcast* all about perfectionism and the good/bad binary, Mally asks us to all consider:

'What if I knew my inherent worth? What if I knew that I am inherently valuable and lovable and worthy and needed and important in this world? What if that's the foundation that I do my unlearning from, the foundation I do my activism from . . . that way we can't ignore discomfort, but it's no longer connected to my inherent worth.'[77]

Under this idea, being wrong about something should not cause us to crumble in response. We would have space to really understand what is being said by whatever or whoever is challenging us, rather than jumping to an emotional and defensive response. We would have that space because our sense of self-worth would have a firm foundation.

What I find most helpful about viewing fragility that way is that it gives grace for the fragility. It does not come from spite, or hatred of something different or other. Instead, it comes from wider systems which lead us to question our worth and be unwell in far too many ways. So whilst being able to heal ourselves can help heal the system, we are clear that the actual problem is the system that is making us unwell. Therefore, whilst our own healing is important, we have to tackle the system that is causing the harm in the first place. There is also so much more to be said about the importance of community healing, and how insidious it is that capitalist individualisation makes us unwell and then tells us to fix ourselves alone, something that we'll go on to explore in Chapter 9.

I used to believe that changing the world relied on changing hearts and minds. If only enough people knew about the intensity of climate breakdown, oppression and suffering happening in the world, then we would be able to take down the systems causing all of it. That we just had to win over enough individuals and that would cause a landslide. It took me a while to recognise that it's not all about knowledge. People can know things and still not change their behaviour.

Reading Olufemi Taiwo's[‡‡‡‡‡] writing about the 'common ground' in *Elite Capture* made me realise that it's about much more than just hearts and minds – it's about changing how and if people *act*. On this Taiwo writes: 'The point was not just to change hearts and minds, but to change the *common ground* – to change what information was *usable* by people in their daily interactions.'[78]

‡‡‡‡‡ I've referenced a few of Taiwo's books in this book because his work is brilliant. Please do check it out. Especially the chapter on the common ground in *Elite Capture*.

So what is the 'common ground'? The common ground is similar to the Overton Window that we talked about before, but rather than this being about policy decisions, it's more focused on how we act in our daily lives. It's based on what *all* of us do, rather than just what governments do.

The common ground is the information that we as a society deem to be widely known, true and accepted by all; the things deemed as common sense that then dictate what is a reasonable way to act. It includes simple things like the fact that we should walk on a pavement rather than in the middle of the road. The important thing to understand about the common ground is that people don't have to believe in the ideas within it to act within the lines it provides. That is to say that you don't have to have a deep love for pavements to choose to walk on them; you walk on them because you know what the consequences of not walking on them could be. In a similar way, many people act in certain ways and uphold oppressive systems not because they deeply believe in them, but instead, it seems far more likely that they act the way they do because they are afraid of the consequences for not staying within the proverbial lines of these systems. In Taiwo's words:

'Understood this way, common ground is just the informational aspect of the social environment that we build and rebuild with words and deeds. And when we successfully challenge the common ground, we are changing the social environment itself.'[79]

All of this is to say that we cannot just focus on our own personal unlearning if we want to create a better world. We can't just wait and hope for everyone to get up to speed with the same level of understanding. We have to share our knowledge, talk to each other, challenge the systems that dictate the common ground and make ideas and actions based in justice for all – such as joining a union and being involved with organising – common sense. Bringing these into the common ground is what will make a much bigger impact.

Using this understanding of the common ground, we can see why more people don't challenge the ideals they have been raised with. Rather than it being that people hold deep white supremacist or capitalist beliefs, it is far more likely that they are scared of the social consequences of admitting change and previous wrongdoing. Whilst this won't be true for everyone, it is important to consider. In this respect, it is essential for us to create an environment where people are able to challenge their beliefs, change and still be able to be part of a community in some form. The fear of rejection, the fear of isolation, the fear of cancellation – a term that's come to mean a lot of things, I know – is really holding us back.

Cancel culture isn't new. But I do think that our increased exposure to it is having an impact on our ability to allow ourselves to be wrong and to unlearn. Whilst cancel culture in its inception was about calling for accountability from those in positions of power, it's often used within movement spaces and communities in a more harmful way.

I won't be doing a deep dive into cancel culture here, but what I do want to comment on is how it has impacted each and every of us. The idea that we will be harmed, ousted from our communities or publicly shamed if we step out of line or make a mistake is not the win we think it is. This fear leads to us being unwilling to grow and change – two things that are absolutely necessary for societal transformation. It also leads to distrust in our relationships, as we believe that people are always policing us. Yes, that wording is intentional because this framework also replicates many of the same ideas used in a system that many of us who espouse this behaviour say that we are opposed to: prisons and policing. We cannot use carceral ideas to create freedom and liberation.

Cancel culture thrives on the good/bad binary. There is no allowance for nuance or – dare I say it – humanity. Who is really winning from something that causes great disunity and distrust in our movements?

This all creates a fragility within us that prevents us from being transformed and transforming the world around us. Change quite literally comes from changing our ideas – deciding to leave old ones behind and reach for new ones.

In *We Will Not Cancel Us*,[§§§§§] adrienne maree brown, author and doula, challenges us on the use of cancel culture within out movement spaces:

'We won't end the systemic patterns of harm by isolating and picking off individuals, just as we can't limit the communicative power of mycelium by plucking a single mushroom from the dirt. We need to flood the entire system with life-affirming principles and practices, to clear the channels between us of the toxicity of supremacy, to heal from the harms of a legacy of devaluing some lives and needs in order to indulge others.'[80]

As we continue to delve further into discussions around cancel culture and accountability, keep these words close, from bell hooks, author and feminist activist, in conversation with Maya Angelou in 1998:

'For me, forgiveness and compassion are always linked:

---

§§§§§ This book is a must read. It is SO deeply healing.

how do we hold people accountable for wrongdoing and yet at the same time remain in touch with their humanity enough to believe in their capacity to be transformed?'[81]

I've previously been quite hostile to critiques of cancel culture. I saw many of these critiques as a way for powerful people to evade 'accountability'. I saw the critiques as a protectionist strategy used by individuals to allow for maintenance of existing power. I collapsed all critiques of cancel culture together as a silencing tool against all forms of call outs and accountability. In this sense, I had equated accountability with punishment, rather than with growth and meaningful change for our movements.

Over time, I began to recognise how at odds some of my values – especially my abolitionist ones – were with some of my actions. I recognised how quick I was to join in with the mob mentality, to gossip and tear down.****** How often I would say, 'Normalise changing your opinion when presented with new information', yet would not give space for others to have that opportunity. In jumping to cancel some folks within my own movements before seeking understanding, mediation or opportunity for transformation, I eventually recognised I was espousing similar beliefs to those that uphold the carceral and prison industrial system and supremacy ideals. I was enforcing a good/bad binary. I would talk about the harm caused by systems but then would pick off individuals as some sort of solution.

So how do we actually incorporate accountability? We can't just leave it behind, right?

Accountability is still so important and harm still has to

****** I remember clearly one day a friend said that maybe we should start keeping a spreadsheet of who's 'cancelled' so that we don't forget and end up being cancelled ourselves. I remember considering it...

be addressed, otherwise we won't be able to have real justice. Being aware of power dynamics is of course essential, and in this instance I'm talking about how we react to other people within our movements, rather than towards politicians, CEOs or those who have significantly differing levels of power than us.

As people who want to build new worlds, rather than just clinging onto the corpse of the old one, we need to find ways of holding people accountable that do not replicate the same systems we say we are against. Using transformative-justice ideals, we must not pursue punishment but instead transformation of the situation. Accountability and punishment are two different things. We must focus on what we want to get out of the situation and how we want to move forward, rather than just replicating and continuing to perpetuate harm.

On this, brown says:

'That's why our way forward isn't to dismiss call outs, or to urge people to stop. No, our words are powerful and are meant to be heard. The way forward is to forge abolition with both hands in the dirt, building empathy in the mirror; it's to remember that innocence is never a prerequisite for human dignity, nor for human rights and freedom; that the words we speak aloud offer prediction for what will be, and must therefore manifest not our smallest vision for the world, but our biggest.'[82]

With this in mind for our movements, rather than jumping to form mobs and tear down, I think we should endeavour to actually work through the issues we have with each other. Where possible, when disagreements happen within movement spaces or with peers, how can we try to facilitate conversations or processes that will actually result in transformation of the situation at hand. Perhaps normalising mediation for conflict resolution in our spaces could be a start.[††††††]

I didn't use to be so comfortable with discomfort, and there are definitely times when I can still feel fragile when challenged, but I'm getting better at it. Strangely, one of the things that helped with this was wild swimming. I was told that cold-water swimming is good for you because it gets you used to discomfort. It can help with anxiety and reduce fear. The cold can feel so shocking at first that it can seem like pain, but the more you do it, the better it gets, and you realise that the pain you felt was actually just discomfort.

Hearing about this, in November 2020, at the start of a cold Scottish winter following eight months of lockdown, half of which I'd spent on placement on a Medicine of the Elderly ward as part of my medical training, I decided to give it a go.

I'd taken myself up north from Edinburgh to Loch Lomond for a break. Being surrounded by nature was a blissful release from the stress coming from all angles.

To be frank, I didn't want to go in the loch when it came to it. This was meant to be a break from stress, and the idea of willingly making myself freezing felt counterintuitive. In all honesty, I was afraid. I definitely squealed when my foot hit the cold loch water. But when I came out I felt absolutely fucking invincible. The way it forced all of my muscles to tense up meant that afterwards I felt more relaxed than I'd felt in ages. I even went in again the following day. Each time was easier than the last. That year, 2020, had brought me a lot of discomfort – some of it the necessary kind – and

---

[††††††] adrienne maree brown has a bunch of resources on abolitionist conflict resolution and accountability practices on their 'Emergent Strategy' website.

all of it led me to fear any discomfort a little less. It encouraged me to step into the discomfort, the fear, the challenge, a bit more. All in the hope that the next discomfort would be even easier and that change would come.

I believe that the same is true of the discomfort that comes with opening yourself to being wrong about something and changing based on new information. I know that none of this is easy or comfortable. Whilst a new world is possible, there will be some discomfort along the way, and we need to be OK with that. As with cold-water swimming, each time will be easier than the last.

But far too often we confuse this discomfort with pain. They are different things. Pain is our body telling us to stop doing something. It's our body saying to stay the fuck away from that thing, because it will hurt you.

Discomfort is different. Discomfort comes from our understanding of things being challenged.

When we aren't used to discomfort, it can feel similar to pain. We can want to jump away from whatever it is.[‡‡‡‡‡‡] Being able to recognise the difference here is essential if we want a better world, and if we want to create change.

Change in many ways starts with us. *We* are society. If we want it to change, we will also have to change. Discomfort is a necessary part of change. Discomfort is *necessary* in a white-supremacist, hetero-cis-normative, ableist patriarchy. The type of discomfort necessary is one that challenges the norms you've been taught about this world. It works out and examines the impact of these norms on people's lives.

It's not just about other people; it's about each and every

---

‡‡‡‡‡‡ For listeners to *The YIKES Podcast*, this is what I mean by 'YIKES and run away' . . .

one of us too. If we aren't willing to change and be transformed, how do we expect anyone else to be? How do we expect the world to be? We have to create room for change. We must.

Challenges to these norms can be so scary that we just want to run away from them or ignore them. But we can't. We can't allow ourselves to. Because absolutely everything – and I literally mean that, given the immensity of the climate crisis – is riding on us transforming the world, and the systems that it's comprised of, for the better. I hope that we will all be brave enough to do it.

There is an infinite amount to unlearn and learn about climate justice. It is a lifelong journey. Rather than scaring us, that should excite us. As we go through our lives doing the important world-building work that is so necessary, we will be transformed too. When we are transformed, we transform the world around us. Unlike caterpillars who only get to do their butterfly transformation once, we get to do it over and over and over. Each time is easier and more beautiful than the last – but only if we keep our ears open to listen and hearts open to be moved.

So, do the learning and unlearning. Read theory if that works for you, have conversations and learn from your community, but don't do it alone. Share what you're learning with those around you.

Don't limit your 'work' to *just* learning and reading and understanding more. Whilst all of this is important, we have to focus on impact too. Learning about an issue is not enough. Having 'good politics' is not enough. This work isn't about reaching individual enlightenment or self-improvement. We have to do what good politics asks of us: join movements and actively organise for a liberated future.

8. THAT'S NOT THE TYPE OF DIVERSITY WE WANT

We don't think you fight fire with fire best; we think you fight fire with water best. We're going to fight racism not with racism, but we're going to fight with solidarity. We say we're not going to fight capitalism with black capitalism, but we're going to fight it with socialism.'

—Fred Hampton, Chairman of the Illinois Chapter of the Black Panther Party

During my sabbatical year from medical school, I lived in Colombia for three months around a pivotal election in that country's history. It was an exciting time to be there. After two hundred years of right-wing elite rule, there was real, tangible hope for transformation if the Pacto Historico candidates – a historic pact of the left-wing coalition – were elected to government. Before the result of this most recent election, many headlines read 'Colombia Will Soon Have a Black Vice President'. Often, this outcome was depicted as hopeful: the fact that both of the final two parties had Black women as running mates is an indication of progression in a country, right?

The two women, Francia Márquez and Marelen Castillo, could not be more different. Whilst Márquez – a former houseworker, teen parent and a climate-justice and feminist activist from the age of thirteen – was running on a politics based on tackling racism and classism at the root to improve the material conditions of life for the majority of Colombians, Castillo was running on a politics of inclusion into the existing system, with more opportunities for women to get higher-paying jobs. Márquez's campaign was for a transformed society that tackled the root causes of oppression, whereas Castillo's campaign merely called for more women to assume the oppressive roles that are currently occupied by men. One was a politics that would actually improve the lives of oppressed Black people in Colombia, the other was a politics that intended to potentially allow a few Black people to become the oppressor. But still, many collapsed all of this to imply that both candidates being Black women would mean that they would both result in liberation or progress for Black people.

Castillo also appeared seemingly out of nowhere as the running mate for Rodolfo Hernandez – the right-wing presidential candidate referred to as 'Colombia's Trump'. Many suggested that, in seeing the popularity of Francia Márquez, Rodolfo wanted to weaponise and take on the prospect of a Black vice-president for himself. He wanted to use Castillo's Blackness as a pawn to gain voters.

This is a key instance in which identity politics was weaponised to uphold the status quo and existing power structures, rather than challenging them. Now that we're all OK with challenging our ideas about things after the last chapter, it feels like a good time to get into this discussion.

The origins of the term 'identity politics' come from the Combahee River Collective's Statement. The Combahee River Collective was made up of Black, queer women organisers who had felt that, in the face of patriarchy within movement spaces and the reality that Black women's liberation was then and still is persistently ignored, they were unable to bring their full selves into their politics. The Black, queer women organisers in the collective – which included the revolutionary poet Audre Lorde, whose work I lean on often – experienced opposition to addressing their particular needs as Black, queer women in both the white feminist movement and the civil-rights movement. They argued that Black women have a right to formulate their own agenda based upon the material conditions they faced as a result of race, class, gender and sexuality. Identity politics was about including radical Black feminism into the politics they were organising around and for. It was created as an emergency response to the specific and persistent harm and exclusion faced by Black women, and to prioritise the radical liberation of *all* Black people, rather than just the liberation of Black men: a politics of unity and collective liberation, rather than division. I am grateful for the ways that the Combahee River Collective's work has positively shaped our movement spaces.

Unfortunately, today identity politics (IdPol) is often removed by many from its radical beginnings and is weaponised by the right wing, who claim to oppose it whilst thriving on using it for 'divide and conquer' politics, or by elites who knowingly or unknowingly use it to 'get ahead'. Instead of IdPol being about truly collective liberation, aspects of it have been morphed into a shallower 'inclusion politics', which simply pursues inclusion or surface-level representation of different identities in different fields or the media. Rather than ripping up the roots of oppressive systems, this version simply makes cosmetic amendments to allow the same system to adapt. It has come to be used as a way to sell an individualised, false liberation: monetary wealth and power within oppressive systems.

Inclusion politics has often actually got in the way of genuine progress. Being seen to have diverse representation has been prioritised over any real changes being made, such as resisting or abolishing existing systems of oppression. Rather than challenging the foundations of these systems toward true liberation, this focus on representation alone has made inclusion into existing systems the goal. As Emma Dabiri puts it in *What White People Can Do Next*: 'Inclusion is access to power in a system that is ultimately a tool of destruction.'[83]

I understand why we might aim for inclusion – once that was all that I aimed for too. But I hope that by this point in the book, you are already recognising that to make inclusion the end goal is to limit the possibilities available to us. I really believe that we can push for better than what Dr Martin Luther King Jr referred to as 'integrating into a burning house'. We must push for collective liberation.

With all of that said, it would be remiss of me, as a young Black girl who grew up in almost exclusively white environments, not to say that of course representation *can* matter, but it is not the be all and end all. I know how much seeing someone who looks like you in the media or in a job in a positive light can transform how you see the world. I definitely cried a lot at the videos of elderly and infant Afro-Colombian people saying, '*La vicepresidenta se parece a mi!*' ('The vice president looks like me!') following Francia Márquez's election; squealed when Tiana in the 2009 *The Princess and The Frog* and Halle Bailey's 2023 Ariel gave little Black girls princesses they could dress up as; and sobbed when watching *Black Panther*.

It was never seeing Black doctors when I was growing up, as well as learning about the amount of medical racism that exists, that made me go to medical school to try and change that in the first place. Then, as the only Black medical student in my cohort at university, with not a single Black person on the leadership team of the medical-school staff, I experienced the impacts of a severe lack of diversity. It was four years into my degree before I even met another Black doctor on placement or in teaching, and when I did, I actually cried. It really meant a lot to know that I wasn't alone.[§§§§§§] I can say with absolute certainty that this lack of representation is a significant part of why my time at medical school was so traumatising; why I experienced racism so frequently, and why, when I raised serious concerns, no real change happened. I often wished that the leadership would change for the better.

But, I have to say that, despite believing in my soul that things would have been different for me if there had been greater, more meaningful diversity in the leadership team, I still don't see that as a complete solution. Representation matters, but it is not the only thing that matters. In an institution such as medicine, which has been built upon ideals of whiteness and white supremacy, we can't undo all of

---

[§§§§§§] Big shoutout here to Dr Sonia, who has been a huge support to me.

the harm it perpetuates by just changing who is at the top. The change has to be deeper than that.[*******]

Whilst I really understand the well-meaning intention of simply switching out those currently in power with racially minoritised people, it severely misunderstands the systemic nature of oppression. It fails to recognise the fact that oppression is in the foundations of many of the systems that exist today and therefore simply changing who is at the top does not fix the fact that the system itself requires there to be people at the bottom.

Outside of these sorts of organisations, representation and inclusion politics also run wild on social media. Online, we are often surrounded by celebrations of more diverse advertising campaigns by inherently exploitative brands. Fast-fashion companies, shoe brands and more have managed to quieten criticism over their continued exploitation of working-class women of colour in the Global South by making their brands look more inclusive through advertising campaigns. These brands will give pay cheques to influencers and public figures that amount to more than any of their garment workers make in a lifetime, with the aim of presenting their brand as one that cares about the collective interests of the global majority. This phenomenon has been referred to as 'ethical-washing'. By doing so, these brands and companies aim to direct our attention away from the reality of the exploitation ingrained in their business models, pacify us within these systems, and thereby distract us from pursuing true liberation.

******* *Inflamed: Deep Medicine and the Anatomy of Injustice* by Raj Patel and Rupa Marya addresses this all in depth.

As Emma Dabiri so rightly puts it, 'the revolution will most certainly not be "diversity in advertising campaigns"',[84] but as a Black woman I also understand why so many of us get sucked into this idea of wanting to 'secure the bag' or get to the top, given that this has so often been withheld from us more than anyone else. As people, we want a few simple things: to be loved, to be happy and to be secure. We are all submerged in a capitalist society that tells us that in order to have these things we must always be striving for *more*. This society tells us that there is no security unless you have excess. We are forced to believe that we must keep climbing our way up the proverbial ladder. We internalise the idea that we just have to look out for ourselves. Collectively, we are taught to ignore the exploitative reality that, under capitalism, for wealth to be generated for those at the top, it is being extracted from somewhere and someone else. We are often made to believe that there isn't another way; that the way the world is is just how it's always going to be and that we simply need to do our best within it. As Black women in particular, as we have historically and continually had so much taken or kept from us, we are often forced into a scarcity mindset to an even greater extent. We – and I say 'we' because, at different times in my life, I have also fallen into this way of thinking – perhaps saying, 'oh, but a cisgender, heterosexual white dude will demand and get *x* amount of wealth or power, so why can't I?' The key thing to hold onto here is that we don't want diversity in who gets to be the oppressor. We want oppression to be gone.

I don't simply want a world in which Black women, for example, get to occupy the spaces currently filled by white men; I want a world where *no one* occupies that much power or has a monopoly on power over others; where no one is exploited and harmed – no matter who gets to benefit from the results of that. Our liberation exists *outside* of capitalism, existing hierarchies and power structures. We deserve better.

We need to really remind ourselves of how interconnected we all are – how connected all of our experiences are. People are made poor by resources being kept from them, and others become rich through hoarding those resources. Whilst pursuing becoming a girlboss, 'Black capitalist' or getting to the top *might* benefit you now in the form of monetary wealth, it can only be achieved at the expense of those who are exploited, those who have less so that you can have more. In the system that we live in, for one person to make it to the top, there are a bunch of workers of all racialised identities whose wages are kept low, whose agency is removed and have profits kept away from them, and the climate crisis is perpetuated. Whilst capitalism and neoliberalism might have made us believe that we are all separate from each other, that is not the case. Our lives are all intertwined. Our liberation is dependent on each other. We have to remember this.

We also have to dismantle the idea that achieving or accessing the benefits that come from being at the top of these hierarchies will result solely in positive outcomes for the person there. In her essay 'Class, Privilege and Loss' in *Medicine Stories*, Aurora Levins Morales writes about the loss that comes with accessing 'privilege':

'In order to access upward class mobility, these groups were required to surrender vibrant relationships of solidarity with Indigenous communities and communities of color, particularly African Americans, betray friends and neighbors, and accept the mistreatment of those people as being in some way justified. Because of the very insecurity of the privileges offered, these groups were persuaded to narrow their circle of self-interest and accept the exclusion of People of Color.'[85]

Morales is speaking to the loss that occurs when one is able to scale up the proverbial class ladder and gain privilege or benefits within this current system – for example, as the result of moving from being positioned as a worker to being a boss and the increase in capital and power that comes along with that. This change in positionality, which would come with an increase in access to capital or money, would require a letting-go of connection to those who are exploited to generate that capital. In this way, privilege indeed has a cost too. This cost is of course not equated with the violence and lack experienced by the oppressed at the bottom of this hierarchy, but it is so important that we acknowledge that even in privilege, there is something lost. To choose to have personal gain at the expense of other fellow human beings, animals and nature is to really detach oneself from one's own humanity. It's toxic. But within this system, it can feel like the greatest aspiration available to us.

The longer we uphold these oppressive systems, the longer we allow them to adapt and survive and remain relevant by 'diversifying' them without changing their fundamentally oppressive structures, the longer it will be before we can get to something better. We all deserve something better. We all owe our fellow humans something better.

We can't solely focus on how things look; we have to focus on the visions that are being included, and we need to focus on what the material outcome of these changes will be.

This is why it is so essential for us to have an understanding of 'whiteness' – as discussed in Chapter 3. An understanding of 'whiteness' gives us an understanding of power structures. This understanding of power structures allows us to go beyond weak analyses which just focus on what we can see and instead focus on what the impacts of any given actions will be on the lived experiences of the people at the bottom of a system of oppression and power.

We need to ask ourselves: *what does this do for the material conditions of the people at the bottom of a system of oppression and power? Does this improve their living conditions and rights, and move us towards a climate-just society? Or could it possibly be that this actually holds us back from all of those things?*

In 2022, in the midst of complete chaos, the racist, homophobic prime minister Boris Johnson was finally forced to resign by a revolt from his own party. The leadership race that followed was dubbed by some international commentators as 'progress', given that the majority of those running were not racialised as white. We had Kemi Badenoch, previous Equalities Minister, who downplayed the existence of systemic racism. Rishi Sunak, the previous Chancellor of the Exchequer and richest MP, whose billionaire wife didn't even pay full taxes in the UK before it became a scandal. Sajid Javid, who made history as Home Secretary by setting a precedent for revoking citizenship of a British national in the case of Shamima Begum, a young girl trafficked to Syria by a Canadian agent. Suella Braverman, who as Attorney General referred to the act of migrating to the UK via dinghies as 'stupid'.[86] The cherry on the diverse top of the fascist cake was Priti Patel, then Home Secretary and implementer of the most violent immigration policy the UK has had in living memory, with her plan to send those seeking asylum to Rwanda being denounced by the United Nations Human Rights Commission as violating international law.

What the actions of this so-called diverse collection of politicians shows us is that representation and inclusion alone can be a shallow politics if we do not look any further than that. We must ask who is actually being represented by the actions taken and who those in power – no matter their identity – are held accountable by. Shaista Aziz, Labour councillor and anti-racism campaigner, elaborated on this in response to celebrations of this diversity: 'It's not enough to be a Black or ethnic minority politician in this country or a cabinet member. That's not what representation is about. That's actually tokenism.'[87]

All but one of these candidates dropped out as the race narrowed down to two: Rishi Sunak and Liz Truss. The new prime minister would either be a woman from a working-class background or a person of colour – progress, right?

During the race, Sunak released a video where he said this:

'I know what racism is: I've experienced it myself. So I want to be clear with you all – there is absolutely nothing racist about wanting Britain to have secure borders that work. In fact, those immigrants who came here legally are the first to say: "We played by the rules; why should other people get away with breaking them?"'[88]

Sunak used his racialisation as a person of Indian descent to defend policies that cause disproportionate harm and violence to people racialised just as he is. Borders necessitate violence in being upheld and the UK government's 'Hostile Environment' policy – a term they coined themselves – is a clear example of that.

Sunak is basically saying, 'Hey, I look like these people and therefore I must be advocating for them, so trust what I say.' In actual fact, he is using his heritage and racialisation to condemn people who are also racialised as people of colour to violence in detention centres, death as a result of being forced into unsafe routes of travel to gain asylum, and increased trauma. Who is it that benefits from these so-called secure borders? It's absolutely not the global majority. It's a small minority at the top of our power structures who can continue to use migrants and refugees as scapegoats, rather than adequately addressing Britain's colonial and continued role in their displacement in the first place. Sunak's vision, words and actions are for that elite, rather than the global majority, or even for people who look like him. There really couldn't be a clearer example of how identity politics can be weaponised by the elites to dismiss criticism and maintain power structures.

In a similar way, some have argued that Priti Patel was put in charge of the Home Office to inhibit criticism of the abhorrent racism it perpetuates. In the time Patel was in this role, the UK government made the situation even more hostile and deadly for those without leave to remain. Patel has worked to dehumanise and demonise migrants and refugees. No safe routes to gain asylum are available, forcing people like three-year-old Alan Kurdi to travel via routes which all too often prove fatal. Those who do manage to make it to the UK and claim asylum are prevented from working, deliberately sent far away, and isolated from friends or family and forced to live off a weekly £40.85 for each person in a household. Life is deliberately made incredibly difficult, and people are intentionally left in a state of limbo in the hope that it will 'deter' people from coming.[†††††††]

The culmination of this was the infamous 'Rwanda plan' mentioned earlier; a truly horrifying reality. It really is

[†††††††] I really recommend watching the film *Limbo* (2020), directed by Ben Sharrock, to understand the experience of those seeking asylum.

astounding that, despite Patel's legacy being her implementations of the most aggressive policies that negatively impact communities of colour, some have still suggested that her very position is an indicator of progress against racism. In fact, the only door opened by her appointment was for her successor, Suella Braverman, to be even worse.

If anything, I believe that the progress of elitist people of colour who implement racist policies into positions of power can be more of a hindrance to liberation than a white person assuming that role. 'Diversifying' a system without changing anything about the structural oppression of it simply allows this harmful system to adapt for longer, to appear improved, seem more relevant and evade necessary criticism. We really have to look beyond what is visible to us and analyse what this really means for the people who need change most.

In his book *Elite Capture: How The Powerful Took Over Identity Politics (And Everything Else)*, Olúfémi O. Táíwò terms this phenomenon 'elite capture': 'Elite capture happens when the advantaged few steer resources and institutions that could serve the many towards their own narrower interests and aims.'

He goes on to say:

'We should respond to the problems of elite capture, and the racial capitalism that enables it, not with deference politics but with constructive politics. A constructive approach would focus on outcome over process: the pursuit of specific goals or results, rather than mere avoidance of "complicity" in injustice or promotion of purely moral or aesthetic principles. A constructive approach fits squarely into what political theorist Michael Dawson calls "pragmatic utopianism . . . that starts where we are, but imagines where we want to be", combining a set of goals unbound by whatever passes for common sense today with a "hardheaded political realism" capable of finding the strategies and tactics needed to shift common sense and the world underneath it.'

Rather than focusing on what 'who's at the table' looks like – that is, on what Morales refers to as 'cosmetic inclusion' – we have to ask whose visions are present in that space. There could be a table that's filled with racially minoritised folks like Rishi Sunak, Priti Patel and Kemi Badenoch, which might appear to be better for our collective liberation than a table that's just occupied by white folks, but the real impact of that cosmetic inclusion on people's lives is absolutely not a guarantee. The visions present are more important than only what is visible.

Of course, I am still a huge advocate for having increased meaningful representation in every space that can push us towards liberation. As I've written about before, there is often a profound lack of diverse peoples and perspectives in the climate-justice space. It's incredibly unlikely that a leadership just filled by white people would be effective in advocating for and understanding the visions of global-majority communities. That's because it is true that privilege – and that means all types of privilege: financial, racial, class, gender, educational and more – obscures our view of the world. The limitations of our lived experiences can often prevent us from understanding an issue as well as someone with lived experience of it. If you have not lived a life being oppressed by interpersonal and systemic racism, it is likely that there will be many parts of living that experience that you won't know or understand as well as someone who has. This is why I think that reading, having conversations, using social media or podcasts or any other form of storytelling available to you is so important. When we listen to and learn from each other, our view of the world becomes clearer. The way that privilege can obstruct us from being able to see a way out, a better future, is lessened by understanding more and more about each other.

At the same time, though, just because you have had certain experiences does not guarantee that the vision for the future you are working towards is one that tackles those issues at their root.

Having people who have lived experience of being oppressed is of vital importance, but only if they are bringing the visions of liberation for the oppressed with them.

All that being said, I do want to make a note here about the overemphasis on lived experience as a qualifier. There has been a tendency in social-justice spaces to say that we must pivot to and focus on getting those who have experienced deep trauma at the hands of oppressive systems to become the leaders in tackling these issues. This pivot and focus is the result of the fact that, for too long, the leadership within movements and the people given power and responsibility to create change have been overwhelmingly white and male. It's well meaning, and I really am so grateful that efforts are being made to prioritise perspectives that for far too long have been shoved to the side or ignored.

My concern is the pressure that can be placed on those who have been traumatised to not only find a way to navigate the harm that trauma does to both our bodies and minds, but also to be the ones to lead the conversations and find a way out. Rather than standing beside those who have been traumatised in solidarity and supporting them, the call has instead become to platform them; elevating them above everyone else. It's an immense amount of pressure.

Moreover, I question the idea that holding liberatory ideals, having empathy and wanting to build something better are only characteristics you can have if you have experienced oppression, trauma and violence. This just further glorifies suffering, something which can inhibit our movements. I want to believe that empathy is our default response as humans. Our default as people is to connect with and love each other. It is the oppressive systems around us that have worked to separate us and chipped away at our innate ability to experience empathy. The only thing that is different in this respect for oppressed people and people on the margins is that the experience of oppression can create a more lucid understanding of how the oppressive systems work.

So, having unpacked all of that, what *is* the kind of diversity we should be working towards? What sort of representation matters? The diversity we are seeking is one that will actually create a world that is fundamentally different, better and more liberated for all peoples – rather than one that just *looks* more inclusive.

We need to work towards a diversity that leads to a safer, more dignified, more joyful, healthier world for all of us – but especially for those currently most oppressed in this world.

The kind of diversity we want is one where no one's struggle is too big, no one is a distraction, none of us are forced to permanently leave our own liberation behind to fight for someone else's, but rather we recognise the interconnectedness of all of our liberations, in order to expand our visions and fight for more.

The kind of diversity we want will be led by those whose experiences and imaginations can work together and combine to move us towards the futures that we need. We need to implement representation that *actually* represents the people – especially those who have been historically excluded. I say 'futures' here because we are going to need more than one. We need futures that honour all of the experiences of oppressed peoples. We need futures that encompass the breadth of our hopes and dreams for a better world.

The kind of diversity we want is about strengthening and improving the collective, rather than just platforming an individual.

The kind of diversity we need is a diversity of ideas about how to navigate our way out of this climate crisis, a diversity of tactics for building a new world and disrupting oppressive systems; a diversity of skills to be used in movements to build change. This diversity will come from a collective of those whose voices have historically been silenced and every voice that adds itself to theirs.

9. HEROES WON'T SAVE US, BUT COMMUNITY WILL

'It is essential to resist the depiction of history as the work of heroic individuals in order for people today to recognise their potential agency as a part of an ever-expanding community of struggle.'

—*Angela Davis, Freedom is a Constant Struggle*

Growing up, I never thought I could be an activist. Perhaps you too have felt or still feel that way. Where I was raised, the only activists I had heard about were people like Nelson Mandela, Dr Martin Luther King Jr., Harriet Tubman, Nanny of the Maroons and Malcolm X. I learned about exceptional individuals.

I thought that, to be an activist, you had to be an exceptional individual. Like so many of us, in my history classes I was told that activists were people from the past; that the demands of liberation movements had already been fought and won by others who came before me. Hurrah! We were told that all we had to do now was to be grateful that we lived in this Golden Age of Freedom™.

I sensed that this wasn't true. With my own eyes, I could see there was still oppression to resist today, but I didn't really know how to go about it. I didn't know any 'activists' personally. I didn't know then that we all have so much value to contribute to movements. Then I went to Calais to volunteer with a young organisation started by students, now known as Choose Love. In Calais I met real-life activists who, whilst obviously selfless, wonderful and inspiring, were just normal people. They had seen an issue and decided to do something about it. They weren't perfect. They were just seemingly ordinary people who had done extraordinary things. It became clear to me that that was all it took to be an activist: just being active.

We don't need everyone to be a Dr Martin Luther King Jr. or an Angela Davis. We don't need to leave it all to these exceptional individuals. We need movements. As Andre Henry, author, organiser and musician, said, 'We all need to become part of the sleeping giant that awakes.'[89] For me, taking action in Calais felt like finally waking up from a deep sleep of inaction.

The Civil Rights movement of the 1960s was about much more than Dr King and Malcolm X. The struggle against apartheid was about much more than Nelson Mandela. The climate movement is about much more than Greta Thunberg or me or any other climate activist you are already familiar with. Whilst all of these people have undeniably made a huge impact and played pivotal roles in creating a better world for all of us, this focus on exceptional individuals disempowers us from recognising the fact that we are *all* important. This focus distracts us from the reality: that collectives made up of hundreds, thousands, even millions of ordinary people are what drive the greatest change. Active movements drive change.

We must resist these individual-hero narratives because they are, quite simply, false. For any action or change to happen, the work of thousands of ordinary people is going on behind the scenes. There are people who write press releases; people who do research; people who provide well-being support and make cups of tea; people who give legal advice and manage social media; people who sort out logistics and organise finance. This list isn't by any means exhaustive. Actions and campaigns don't just spring up out of nowhere – they require a huge workforce with a wide variety of skills. All of these roles are valuable. It's so much more than people on the streets or behind a megaphone.

Movements are made up of many different people with different roles coming together in order to create change. We need everyone to be active against systems of oppression. We need everyone to join movements for change. We need everyone to be active in the fight for climate justice, and that includes you. So why are we told that change just comes from heroes? Who does this narrative serve?

This obsession with individualism is a product of our capitalist system and – more recently – neoliberal ideology. This ideology tells us that we are in constant competition with each other, that community is dead and that we can and should only rely on ourselves. These individualist ideals are what mean that we will pursue our own success and believe that it is not connected to the lives of others around us.

This idea that we are all separate from each other, that our successes and failures are not intertwined, and that we should tunnel-vision in on our own lives and experiences only works to disempower us from transforming the world. Workers who don't communicate with each other about the conditions they are facing and who do not work together to create change are much easier to control and exploit than a united workforce who will stand together and advocate for one another. It is far easier for the status quo to strip us all of our rights and resources if we are facing them – and their significant institutional power – with only the power of an individual.

Similar to the co-opting of identity politics and the creation of whiteness as a divide-and-conquer strategy, individualism just divides us further to make us alone. When we are sole people, we have less power. We think that it's just us against a big, powerful system; that our losses are inevitable and that the best that we can hope for is to one day assume the place of the people at the top oppressing all of us.

Whilst individualism and divide-and-conquer tactics have been used for centuries, they've become even more prevalent since the proliferation of neoliberalism by Margaret Thatcher in the UK, Ronald Reagan in the US and Augusto Pinochet in Chile.

Alicia Garza sums up the concept of neoliberalism in her book, *The Purpose of Power*:

'Neoliberalism is a series of economic policies and a school of economic thought that resulted in privatization, corporate subsidies, and tax breaks for the wealthy at the expense of working people, the dismantling of the social safety net, and deregulation. Neoliberalism led to the rolling back of the gains won during the last period of civil rights. And it caused devastating destruction to the economy – particularly for workers.'[90]

The most important thing to understand about what neoliberalism has done – for this chapter at least – is to recognise that, as an ideology, it propagates the belief that we are all separate from each other. In a policy sense, unions – one of the biggest forms of collective power and unity – were decimated by the Thatcher era, and union membership has still not recovered, but there were even wider-reaching implications. The constant repetition of ideas from the likes of Thatcher that 'community is dead' and that 'there is no alternative' have invaded and limited the collective imagination. They have made competition the defining characteristic of our relationships to our fellow humans. These ideals have made collective movement building harder. They've caused people to turn away from each other in a crisis, rather than towards one another. I don't think the impact of neoliberal ideology on our collective psychology can be overstated.

Why build walls? Make folks walk single file? Divide and conquer is what it's called!

It's a trap!

No, it's a trial.

Hadestown is a musical all about the power of divide and conquer. I think that it gives a very apt representation of what the combination of neoliberalism and whiteness leaves us all with. Rachel Chavkin, director of *Hadestown* on Broadway, described this so well in her acceptance speech for Best Direction at the Tony Awards:

'My folks raised me with the understanding that life is a team sport. And so is walking out of hell. That's what is at the heart of the show: it's about whether you can keep faith when you are made to feel alone. And it reminds us that that is how power structures try to maintain control: by making you feel like you're walking alone in the darkness, even when your partner is right there at your back.'[91]

We are separated from each other; indoctrinated with individualist ideals and doubt in each other because the status quo is absolutely terrified of the immense power we have to topple elite rule when we come together. With the climate crisis and multiplicity of other oppressive systems facing us, I cannot overemphasise how much individualism will kill us all if we do not resist it. So many are already dying due to it. Imagine the world we could have if we reframed our thinking to see the inherent connections between all of us. It would look very different if we could see ourselves as a part of a wider body rather than walking alone, and if we chose to walk side by side, shining a light through the darkness and working together. The whole world is ours to transform. We can put power back into the hands of the many rather than the few.

The thing is, the promotion of individualist ideals doesn't solely come from those using it in a calculated way to maintain power. It's also pushed by some probably well-intentioned Instagram feminists. I'm sure many of you will have been inundated with social-media posts telling you to 'dump him'; that 'you don't owe anyone anything'; to cut ties with anyone bringing you down and that you should focus your energy on yourself alone. Ash Sarkar, contributing editor for Novara Media, writes about this phenomenon, saying:

'The recognition that the weight of emotional baggage is unevenly distributed has, amongst some contemporary feminists, morphed into the idea that *any* sense of obligation is itself the enemy. There's been a sense of mission-creep from women don't owe you sex, domestic labour, or prettiness to the idea that women don't owe anybody anything.'

Sarkar continues:

'The elasticity of emotional labour as a concept means you can apply it to anything you feel is emotionally taxing, boring, or personally disruptive. Want to learn something? Google it, I'm not your teacher. Need care, love, or support? BetterHelp it, I'm not your therapist. What do we owe to others? Nothing, it seems, other than what's identified as personally nourishing for ourselves. To issue the rebuke of 'not my problem' is a revolutionary act of boundary setting. Self-care is warfare, and all that.'[92]

Whilst I don't believe that these highly individualist narratives are being promoted by these people with negative intentions, and that most of it is said as a response to trauma inflicted on women in a patriarchal society, I still believe that these ideals are dangerous. The reality of this world is that all of our lives are interconnected with each other and with nature, and therefore we have to have a responsibility to each other. Given that whatever we have or don't have in this world is dependent on the actions of other people, we *do* all owe each other so much.

With the multiplicity of crises that humanity is facing, culminating with the climate crisis, responding with a 'not my problem' logic in the face of such issues, and to the suffering of our fellow humans, will not transform our world. It replicates the behaviour and systems of patriarchy. I really believe that we can do better than this.

We must challenge and address the disproportionate weighting of work and care that is based on gender, patriarchy and other forms of marginalisation, whilst also refusing to abandon anyone, or only seeing our social interactions as transactional. We simply don't have to respond to this world with a logic that limits the possibilities for a better world for us all. There are other ways.‡‡‡‡‡‡‡

If you've ever felt alone in trying to challenge this world and its violent norms and instead walk towards and build something better, you are not the only one. If making us feel lonely is one way that the status quo and elites win, then we must fight back by supporting and holding each other. We must build communities and systems of care. We must have each other's backs; we need to remind each other that we are there for each other, always.

There is this belief that a strong, charismatic leader makes a movement strong. But, what if that isn't the case? What if big leaders make our movements more fragile? If the success of our movements and their power is all dependent on one person, then they are only as strong as that one person. They are destined to fail. Because they will only be as strong as one, imperfect human. They will be fragile and break. It's far easier to take down one person than hundreds or even thousands of people within a movement.

Organisers like Alicia Garza, co-founder of Black Lives Matter, have noted that the belief that we need to wait for the next male, charismatic leader to arrive can delay the work getting done. This perception of change being driven by these people, when this is not the reality, can actually delay progress.

‡‡‡‡‡‡‡ There is so much more to say here about the individualisation of care, mental health and more. If you're interested in more on this, I'd recommend reading *It's Not Just You: How To Navigate Eco-Anxiety and The Climate Crisis* by my good friend and fellow climate-justice activist Tori Tsui.

In *The Purpose of Power*, Garza writes:

'Every actor within a social movement has a role to play and contributions to offer that at some point should be recognised. But the pedestals we create for individuals have the opposite effect: They obscure people's contributions. They serve to situate the success of a movement inside one person, as opposed to that success being based on how much a movement grows beyond itself.'[93]

I started writing this chapter from a place of wanting to share my worries and learnings, but I also want to be honest. Given that I have gained a platform and an audience from this work, it is perhaps bizarre to have me writing about the pitfalls of pedestals and individualism. To some, I might be seen as what's called a 'celebrity activist'. Whilst I really don't want to be associated with any of these things, and it's true that a lot of them have caused me harm, it would be false to make out that I've never wanted any of this. It would be untrue to say that I've never pursued it.

Through therapy, I'm working through the 'why' here. Why did I pursue public-facing movement work? Why have I continued with it, even though it continues to bring me distress and harm? Do I just have an absolutely humongous ego that I feed with these platforms?

It's scary being honest, but honesty is important. I think that in a world that has often ground down fundamental parts of myself – my Blackness, my energy for movements and liberation, my unwillingness to settle for what we have already in this world – I yearned to be seen as 'good enough', and even to be celebrated. Growing up as a nerdy but not-nerdy-enough Black girl who loved reading, social justice and silly dancing, I was often kicked down by the almost exclusively white society I was surrounded by. As a result, I continuously strived. Simply being myself wasn't enough to be loved or seen as fully human, and therefore I had to be perfect. Maybe then I would be happy. Maybe that would fix the emptiness inside me. At school, I did this with my grades, then at university I channelled this feeling into organising. It's almost as though I wanted to be perfect at that.

I began writing about my journey on social media, and what started as an account for my friends and family slowly started to grow. Social media is built to be like a game – to be addictive. The emptiness inside of me told me that if I could reach more people with ideas about climate and race then perhaps I would finally be worthy. I would finally feel like I had a purpose. My breath and life would be worth its place on this earth.

At first, the growth of my platform was relatively small. I gradually made it to 8,000 followers on Instagram over a year of actually giving the account some attention and regularly posting. Meanwhile, I was involved in activism on the ground – movement building, action planning and more. Already, I had begun to feel more and more uncomfortable with the fact that I would get full credit for an action that was not my idea or plan, just because I'd done the work of communicating it out to the public. This was all on a relatively small scale, and to be honest, because my platform was so small, more often than not it was white people who would get the credit for the work that had been done by me and my fellow POC organisers. In hindsight, though, I can now see the dangers of pedestals and platforms from that time. I was a twenty-one-year-old activist who got exploited by companies wanting to associate themselves with the climate movement and I fell for it more than once. I let myself believe a lot of the things I warn against in this book. I have learned a whole lot since then.

In 2020, the world locked down due to the coronavirus pandemic and we were all stuck at home. *Cosmopolitan* magazine featured my work in a feature in collaboration with Instagram, and my little account went from 9,000 followers to 30,000 overnight. Followers do not dictate impact, or even meaningful reach, but this sudden growth in my platform was stressful. I was grateful to be able to share my learnings on race and climate with so many more people, but it also felt like my words were suddenly being given more weight simply because a fairly arbitrary number of followers sat beside them. Overnight, it felt as though I was further removed from my own humanity in the perception of others.

A month later, George Floyd was murdered by police officers and the video was shared widely online, sparking the largest resurgence of the Black Lives Matter movement that the world had ever seen. I still can't deeply think about that time without having a physical response to it. My granddad in Jamaica had just passed away and we were unable to attend the funeral due to the lockdown. Social media and the news was filled with videos of Black people being killed and my inbox was full of guilt messages from white people who had caused me harm in my life. For myself and many other Black folks, this entire period was deeply traumatising.

A significant part of this resurgence of activism was occurring in the online space. As most people were locked down, those having their first real awakening to racial justice were looking for answers online. A post I had made when Ahmaud Arbery was brutally murdered just a month before George Floyd started being shared around a fair bit. I was staying off social media as much as possible, as it wasn't a good space for me in my grief.

Then, my follower-count started to rise significantly. I'd been tagged as a good person to follow in some ridiculously viral posts, and guilty white folks were flocking to my account in their hordes. In one week, I went from around 30,000 followers to over 70,000. It really was quite ridiculous. There's so much I could say about the emotional impact all of this had, but for the purposes of this chapter I'm going to focus on the pedestal this following put me on going forward.

I was the same person, with the same skills, ideas and words as I had been just three months before, when only 9,000 accounts followed me, and yet this huge rise in followers led to a dramatic shift in how people interacted with me. My direct messages were a mess of vitriolic hate or complete adoration. There really wasn't anything in between. On reflection, both of these responses indicated that the people sending me those messages didn't see me in the fullness of my humanity.

With a bunch more numbers next to my name, everything I said carried more weight. I was immediately heralded as the leader of movements that I hadn't even organised with on the ground. I was piled on with praise that was disproportionate to the contributions I had made and with hate that was calculated and concerning. Whatever I said was received by many as being the gospel truth, and taken on wholesale, without critical thought, simply because of the platform I had. It felt as though I was constantly being built up and up and up, knowing that one day it would come crashing down, and for some people, it did. If I ever stepped outside the box others had drawn for who I was, folks would try to rip me apart rather than just shrugging it off. It made me scared to live my own life and have my own dreams and needs because they might not fit in with the perfect-activist character that others had curated. In my pursuit of this purist activist perfection, I just enhanced this cycle of pedestalling and perfectionism by striving to be that person that everyone else seemed to see as. This disconnect between who I was – someone imperfect, silly, messy and disorganised – and the perception and expectation that others had for me really wrecked my already-fragile sense of self.

It was as if I had spent my whole life being told that I was never enough, and then one day I was told that in actual fact I was Superman. But every time I tried to run into a phone box to speedily change my clothes, leave behind Clark Kent and emerge in a super-suit with amazing powers, I'd still be Clark Kent. I was still ordinary. I had no magic powers and I was no hero. I was just doing the same work in the same way, at times less often than my comrades and peers who I organised with. There was a disconnect between who I actually was and what others believed.

I began to have frequent panic attacks. I believed I wasn't good enough and had many downward spirals. Impostor syndrome wreaked havoc on my life. I would get piles of praise every day and yet it all made me very unwell.

Whilst this pedestalling – thinking that someone is perfect and can do no wrong – was harming me, I also think it was harming others. Similar to the conversation around perfectionism, the pedestalling of activists just creates more of an 'us' and 'them' narrative. It makes most people believe that they will never be good enough to do anything at all. The idea that an activist has to do no wrong, make no impact on the planet, never, ever fuck up or else be ousted, means that, to many, to be an activist is to not be human. It's to be an ideal. And if you can't be that, why bother trying at all? Leave it to the people who *are* perfect. They'll use their superhuman powers to fix everything for the rest of us.

I think that, to some extent, pedestalling is a comforting thing for those doing it. The existence of superhuman people, of miraculous leaders bringing about change, lets the majority of us off the hook, right? If someone else will come and save us, then we have less to worry about and less to do ourselves. If only superheroes existed. If only someone would fly down from above and fix all of our problems.[§§§§§§§] I'd like that to be true too. But it's just not. And belief in it doesn't help us; it doesn't help the planet; it doesn't help people suffering; and, from my experience, it sure doesn't help the people being pedestalled.

Challenging these pedestals is to say to ourselves, *I'm going to take responsibility for transforming our world, too*. It takes leaning into the necessary discomfort, knowing that it's required in order to transform the world around us. It requires us to lean into and embrace the humanity and interconnectedness of all of our lives. It means taking the blue pill and seeing the world for what it really is and knowing the power each of us has to really transform it.

Acknowledging that the pedestalled person online isn't actually me, but rather a fictional person created by others, has helped me so much. I am no longer as worried or anxious

---

§§§§§§§ I am a person of faith, with faith in the divine and a huge love for Jesus, but I also don't believe that even our faith traditions tell us that we can just sit and wait for God to fix everything. We are called to be active stewards. We are called to be the hands and feet and to build the Kingdom on Earth. We are called to be a huge part of transformation.

about this as I used to be. More than that, though, I've also gained a significant amount of empathy for others. I think this fairly unique experience of being put in the position of 'charismatic leader' has also shown me how often that title isn't really a choice. It has re-humanised people in that position and given me a far more expansive view of how change and movements happen. It reminds me to check my ego every day and to remember the millions of ordinarily wonderful people who never get praise or flowers, but without whom this work would be impossible. This book is my love letter to every single person quietly working to transform the world around us. You are so deeply valued, whether you see it or not. Your work is as important – if not more so – as the work that is more visible.

Visibility is often misleading. In an age of social media, we can celebrate and focus too much on what we can see. What we see isn't everything. Making all the work to create *visible* change isn't always possible. A number of followers or likes or shares does not equate to impact. It's a trick. We have to be mindful of how easy it can be to fall for it.

adrienne maree brown, whose work I have referenced often in this book, shares the importance of cultivating inch-wide, mile-deep relationships over inch-deep, mile-wide relationships. What is meant by this is a focus on critical connections over critical mass – prioritising deeper relationships rather than just reaching as many people as possible. brown says that these deeper relationships, these deeper connections, are what will sustain movements and create transformational change for the long term. Rather than seeing success in numbers, we must see success in what our movements have actually moved.

Of course, for certain things, critical mass is important. To have mass support for an issue can be a key factor in creating change. I want this book to reach as many people as possible. The point here is that this cannot be the sole goal of our movements. Virality can be a distraction from the necessary building work.

For example, if the only goal of this book was to reach as many people as possible, I could tone down and oversimplify climate justice. I could have made this a book that would appeal to everyone. I could hold back all of the challenging and nuanced parts of climate justice and simply make it a book filled with bold, easily shareable statements. But, if it's toned down that much, what's it going to actually do? It wouldn't move people to do anything substantial. In a similar way, if it's too dense and complex, then would it even be helpful for anyone other than those who already care and know about climate justice? That way, I'd just be shouting in a room filled with people who already care, which is also unhelpful.

My aim in writing this book, and what I hope I've done, is to find a way to make these ideas accessible to as many people as possible whilst not toning down or diluting what needs to be said. Sure, this book won't reach every single person on this planet, but I hope that those who do read it and engage with it will have been transformed and pushed into action from it. I hope that, in this way, it can make the most change possible. So please pass this book on to a friend or family member after you've read it. Share what you've learned. Bring other people with you. Get as many people as possible to deeply engage with these ideas.

I think part of our focus on exceptional individuals and charismatic leaders comes from our misunderstanding of how change happens. We see change as the result of short bursts of action, but what we are seeing in those times are just tipping points. From face value, it can seem to us that exceptional individuals like Greta Thunberg or Dr King miraculously mobilise millions overnight. What we don't see is that the sustained, long and often quiet work from millions of ordinary people over generations – many of whom might never have seen the impact of their actions – is what composted the ground to be fertile for these apparent 'miracles'. This generational work builds strong, unseen networks like mycelium do, to allow for the mushroom that is the miracle to grow on the surface. We might only see the mushroom and believe that it came from nowhere, but in fact it is simply the fruit of these vast networks. In this way, they aren't actually miracles at all, but the result of the commitment and work of so many wonderful, ordinary people who decided not to give up. It is this – sustained, consistent organising – that creates the changes we see. Change is a constantly ongoing process. Transformational change requires long work. Often the exceptional individuals – whilst still important – are only the tip of the iceberg.

If you still aren't sold on collectivism, it may be because you believe that it dismisses individuality. This doesn't have to be the case. It's vital to illustrate the difference between individualism and individuality. Individualism tells us that we are alone, that our joy and freedom is separate from the joy and freedom of others. Individualism tells us that we must only look out for our own interests and not the interests of others. Individuality is instead the reality that we are all distinct people; we are all shaped by our experiences to make us unique.

Some have said that the call for collectivism is to remove all appreciation for uniqueness and individuality. It is to say that we should all wish to assimilate into carbon copies of each other and leave behind what makes us unique and different. In this way, some have said that collectivism negates creativity. This is not the case.

The vision of collectivism I am championing in this book is not a future where we are all replicas of each other. It is one where we are all deeply in touch with our unique magic; where we are aware of how our unique experiences have shaped who we are. But it is also a world in which we are aware that what has shaped us is a result of the lives of others around us; others whose lives and unique experiences are inherently connected to ours; an awareness of the reality that we all shape and change each other. Our lives, our joy, happiness and freedom are connected. Rather than collapsing or ignoring what makes each of us unique, collectivism asks us to lean into all of that; to try to understand the stories of all those around us, and the myriad connections. To understand each other and these connections is to understand where we have come from, how we have come to be who we are, and how the world has come to be the way it is. When we understand each other, when we see all of this, it is far easier for us to see where we are going. It requires us to change how we live our lives, as we are aware that the way we live is because of the way others live, and therefore how we choose to act impacts the way others are able to live. To lean into collectivism, to see the similarities in our still-unique experiences, is to find our way out of this. It's to know that none of us are truly free until all of us are free.

One of the biggest problems with the 'hero' activist narrative around movements is that it leads to some people waiting around for a leader to come; waiting to get involved until the point when the new Martin Luther King arises. But we cannot wait for a charismatic or exceptional leader to be deemed popular enough for a mass movement to grow. Liberation cannot wait on a hero. Our collective future cannot be left on the shoulders of an individual.

So many people are not waiting; those who understand that change is a long, sustained process are continuing its long work. The problem is that, whether it's in the headlines or not, there is a lot of work to be done. In the background, the workload is huge. Currently, that huge workload is being shouldered by too few people. It's a recipe for burnout. Yet, for the amount of people who care, the workload is not unmanageable. The problem is the disconnect between many for caring and then actually taking action and taking on some of that work. I truly believe that, no matter when you are reading this book, it's absolutely not too late for you to step up and get involved. We will always need new people, new perspectives and new energy to take on some of the work required to transform the world around us.

Stop waiting. Seriously, stop fucking waiting. You'll be disappointed. Stop expecting someone else to save us – whether it's a hero activist, governments, the scientists or technology. We absolutely cannot afford to wait. We cannot afford to rely on anyone else to save us. We have to realise that the future has to be ours to change ourselves. We have to realise that, when we come together in movements, our collective power increases exponentially. An organised, collective people has far more power than any individual activist. This is such an important thing to understand. As individual people, we can feel powerless in the face of the capitalist system, big corporations and institutions. But when we come together we have so much more power than when we are alone.

After understanding all of the important criticisms of individualism, it's easy to jump to wanting 'leaderless' movements. If charismatic leaders can make movements more fragile, and hierarchy replicates the same power structures that have caused all of this mess, the solution should just be to get rid of leaders, right? I think there's another way we can look at it.

Rather than leaderless movements, we can have leaderfull movements; that is, movements that are filled with many different types of leaders. Spaces where everyone is empowered and given the opportunity to lead in differing ways at different times. Movements that don't replicate the power hoarding that we see in the systems of this world, but instead where power is distributed amongst everyone rather than hoarded by a few. Collectives like that are so much stronger.

I love the idea of leaderfull movements. I came across this concept in the work of Alicia Garza. In *The Purpose of Power*, Garza writes:

'Decentralization would allow for a different practice of power, where many people rather than a small few determined the direction of the project . . . Decentralizing leadership, however, is not synonymous with having "no leaders." Decentralization means distributing leadership throughout the organization rather than concentrating it in one place or in one person or even a few people.'[94]

This idea of redistributing power and leadership amongst organisers was one that revolutionary civil-rights activist Ella Baker was also very passionate about. In an interview about Baker's work, a fellow SNCC activist said this about the leadership that Baker championed:

'Grassroots leadership that will survive even our deaths. So that we are not the leaders. We are organising with local leaders or hoping to develop local leaders because we may not be here and that local organisation has got to survive.'[95]

It is this kind of leadership, disseminated throughout, that makes an organisation so much stronger and more resilient to the inevitable attacks that will come. When we are all empowered to lead in different ways, then our work will outlast any single individual.

The point of this chapter is to say that every single contribution made to this movement matters – public-facing or private, big or small. It makes me so sad to think that folks believe that if they can't do everything then there's no point doing anything at all. The idea that one person should do everything is unsustainable. It's based on ego and it leads to fragile movements. Instead of being reliant on a star player, we need movements where responsibility, work and power is distributed. That way, the work can be sustained for longer and that's how we can be harder to take down.

We've covered the reasons why individualism is bad for movements and why we should join collectives, but for me, the real reason I harp on so much about joining a group isn't just because I think it's the only thing that will really push change. It's also because being in a group means that you'll forge relationships that will support you and keep you going for longer. That makes the work so much more sustainable and long-lasting for ourselves too. Pretty much everything I have learned about climate justice I have learned from being in community with other people; from my wonderful combabes and friends. I quite literally could not do this work without them and their support.

I've spent a lot of my life feeling alone in caring about this stuff. It was only when I joined movements that I realised I'm not alone: none of us are alone in caring this much. There are people who care just as much as you do and these people will hold you and affirm you in caring as much.

Having the audacity to want to see the world as good as it can be is a good thing. It's not 'too much' and it's not something you should 'tone down'. It's something you should hold onto.

There's a quote by the wonderful visionary writer Arundhati Roy that I come back to often. She writes: 'Another world is not only possible, she is on her way. On a quiet day I can hear her breathing.'[96]

In my life, I think it's important to pause, reflect and take notice of where I can hear that breath, and where I can feel it. For me, I feel it most when I'm organising together with other wonderful people in a movement. I've realised more and more that I feel her breathing in movement spaces because, when we come together, to challenge the current world and usher in a new one, we become that breath. We become the new world who is on her way. We get to shape how wonderful she is. Because what is the future if not the result of every single action we all take today?

As I have so often in this book, I want to come back to some words by adrienne maree brown in *Emergent Strategy*:

The future is not an escapist place to occupy. All of it is the inevitable result of what we do today, and the more we take it in our hands, imagine it as a place of justice and pleasure, the more the future knows we want it, and that we aren't letting go.[97]

The challenge of organising and the challenge of building a new world is to find out how we can come together when we fall apart; how to build community in the face of division. It has to be an active choice; we have to choose to turn towards each other's faces, see each other for the fullness of all that we are, even when all we are told to do is turn away. If we don't, our future will be one filled with destruction, but if we can, then the world of our wildest collective imaginations won't be out of reach.

10.
HOPE AS AN ACTIVE STANCE

'Hope is not a lottery ticket you can sit on the sofa and clutch, feeling lucky. It is an axe you break down doors with in an emergency. Hope should shove you out the door, because it will take everything you have to steer the future away from endless war, from the annihilation of the earth's treasures and the grinding down of the poor and marginal . . . To hope is to give yourself to the future – and that commitment to the future is what makes the present inhabitable.'

—Rebecca Solnit, Hope in the Dark

As I write this final chapter, it's nearing the end of summer in the UK. I've returned from nine months living in my birth country of Jamaica and then in Colombia. In both of these places, the persistent and violent legacy of colonialism is impossible to avoid or ignore. In Jamaica in particular, the threat of climate breakdown is evident – as we drove around the island we could see high-water marks on coastal homes that had recently been completely submerged by flooding. Meanwhile, the sea levels are continuing to rise. I thought that coming back to the UK would be a culture shock in many ways, but I also believed that I would be going back to somewhere far away from the worst impacts of this crisis, even though it is in the epicentre of its creation and proliferation.

Just a week after I arrived back in the UK, a heatwave like no other before hit. The UK reached temperatures of forty degrees Celsius for the first time in history. Wildfires broke out all over the country and homes in London even caught alight and burned down. These were temperatures that weren't predicted to happen for almost another thirty years. At the same time, wildfires were decimating many other parts of Europe and the United States, and the worst flooding in living memory was happening in Bangladesh. More than ever before, it became apparent that climate breakdown is here, now and everywhere. We have gone past the point of any part of the globe evading its impacts.

For far too many people, the response to this was to say that it's now too late to tackle this crisis; that we've gone too far and might as well give up. A lot of these responses were no doubt informed by the media posting fatalistic headlines about how 'total climate meltdown cannot be stopped'. Fearmongering was leading to even more inaction.

I know that when I read headlines and articles like this, it doesn't make me want to *do* anything – it makes me fucking terrified. I freeze. I panic. I spiral. Perhaps you experience similar feelings. Whilst all of these responses are valid, they don't move us forward. What *does* move me forward is that climate justice, and solutions based on these principles of tackling the roots of the oppressive systems which have caused this crisis, can offer us a better world for many. What *does* move me forward is hope.

I often get asked what gives me hope. For me, my hope isn't passive or flimsy. It can't be. That's not going to keep me going in the face how completely terrifying everything can be. My hope is based on evidence. It's based on history. It's based on how change has happened before; how worlds have been transformed before, and how they can be again. It's based on the change that millions of ordinary wonderful, loving people have caused through movements like the anti-apartheid struggle in South Africa, the Zapatista movement in Mexico, the Black Liberation movements in the US and so many more.

It's also based on where I can tangibly feel the new world that's on her way, breathing. Like I said, I feel that breath when I'm in organising spaces, surrounded by people who care so deeply that they are giving pockets of their life to try to build a new world. I feel her breath there because we become the breath of the new world when we take the task of creating change into our own hands. We can become the hope we need. We have to.

To fight for the long run, we must find what breaks our hearts and what makes them swell out of our chests. We need to be angry, outraged and saddened by the harm and the violence that comes with the climate crisis and exploitation. We cannot ignore these realities, but we *also* need to find that thing that mends us; the hope for something better that excites us so much that our hearts feel huge and full. Only when we have acquired both anger and hope will we realise that we have no choice but to act in such a way that we will bring about change. We can't help ourselves; the prospect of creating something better is irresistible.

When we are fuelled by outrage alone, our actions aren't sustainable. We run a cycle of reactionary actions, hot takes and short bursts, lacking the sort of stamina required for long, constant, movement-building work.

When we are fuelled only by fear, we risk running into isolationist, individualist ideologies. We risk compromising justice. Or this fear can be all-consuming and lead to defeatism.

These emotions are valid and valuable. I feel them all the time. I've had many climate cries. I've felt fear, heartbreak, outrage and despair. I've allowed myself the space to fall into all of these holes. I've realised that to have a heart that has remained soft, that still breaks in the face of the immense harm that is inflicted on fellow humans all over the world, is to remain in touch with our humanity. These feelings, however hard and painful, are not to be rejected.

I've also felt my heart quicken and swell. I've seen people come together to be the active change we need. I've been reminded that we aren't just fighting to preserve the world as it is; we are fighting to end all oppression and to create something better. We are fighting to end, but also to build.

Before we get into the rest of this chapter, ask yourself this: what breaks your heart and what vision of the future mends it? It's there that you'll find your fight. Despite what we are often told, change is not passive. Sadly, things don't just 'get better' over time. Change is an active process. It's a process that requires participants. It's a process which requires all of us. History shows us this. The future is not set in stone, it is up to us to build it.

I'm not going to sugar-coat things. We have to tell the truth about climate change. False hope won't save us. But active hope can. I base my hope on what has come before us. *Hope in the Dark* by American writer Rebecca Solnit showed me that this type of hope is possible. When we look at the movements for social change that have come before us; when we look at how people have come together to demand change; the fact folks haven't sat on the sidelines but have grasped a new world from the bottom up, I am reminded that we are not the first to do this, and that to hope is to do what they did, to follow in a tradition that has come before us. To learn from their successes – and their failures – and see that we can do that too. We can change the whole world as we know it. But we can only do that if we, well, *do* it. Together, we *can* save so much.

I am hopeful because my ancestors, who were kidnapped from their homeland, chained, shoved into boats, forced to labour day and night, and treated as inhuman, had to believe that their fate was not sealed. They had to believe that the world could be radically transformed. Not only did they have to believe it, they had to *act* with this belief. Hope had to be a verb. They took drastic action, not because they knew they would win but because making the world safer and better is always worth it.

It is because of their active hope that I am here today. I will never know their names or their stories because those too were stolen. But I feel them with me every day. It is their breath in my lungs that I use to speak and shout. It is their blood in my veins that fuels my hands as I write this book and my feet as I march for justice. I still carry their dreams in my mind. If they were able to imagine a way out of a situation that felt so impossible to escape, so can we. So *must* we. We must learn from communities of the present who are surviving against all odds, in the face of powerful opposition, and participate in active solidarity. We must learn from struggles of the past and we must honour them by continuing to push forward and demand better for our future. The necessity to believe in and act on a radical imagination of the future is not new.

There is simply no other way to radically transform the world than to believe in it and do it. Everything can change. *Every single thing can change.* Nothing is immutable. Once you know that – once you believe that everything can change, and that everything that is changed matters – that's when we can transform the world around us. We have always had the power to do that – it simply requires us to realise that and act accordingly.

I am hopeful that as you've made it this far through this book, you are no longer passively reading it. I am hopeful that you have already reached out to your local climate group – or started your own – and have started or continued your organising journey. If you haven't, it's absolutely not too late. It's extremely urgent – and we need to do as much as we can as soon as we can – but it's not too late. In the powerful words of essayist Mary Annaise Heglar: 'If you're worried that it's too late to do anything about climate change and we should all just give up, I have great news for you: that day is not coming in your lifetime. As long as you have breath in your body, you will have work to do.'[98]

The climate-justice movement needs you now and will always need you. We need you because, whether you believe this or not, you have a unique perspective and skills. I assure you that there is a role for you, so please find it. I've scattered a bunch of resources through this book to help you on your way. When times get tough, we don't give up, we get organised.

I can't pretend that my hope is unwavering or easy. But I also know that it's always worth it. Hope is an active choice that we make. Writing this book forced me to have hope every time I sat down in front of my keyboard to write. This process dragged me out of many a doom spiral, and every fibre of my being hopes that reading it might do the same for you.

I know that the only reasonable way to respond to the multiplicity of crises we face is to take them on – to make a plan and work out how we can change everything. You are an important part of that change. So give yourself the space to feel grief, panic and all of the emotions that make complete sense as a way to react to this crisis. But do not allow yourself to fall into nihilism or apathy. Those are completely unacceptable responses. We grieve and then we take action. Because the antidote to climate despair isn't to ignore it all and do nothing; it's to take this issue into our own hands and try to do something about it.

It is not enough to be inspired by other people's actions. True inspiration should move us into action ourselves. It should make you come up alongside activists and do the work with us. To be honest, that is the only way I want anyone to respond to my work. I don't want to hear that I've inspired someone unless that inspiration has made you an active part of movements. Activists and organisers don't do this work to be inspiration porn; none of us are doing this to make you feel like 'we've got it covered' so you can continue as you were. The more people we have, the more the workload will be shared, the happier and healthier our movements can be and the more change we can create. There are currently far too few people carrying the load for all of us and ending up burned out. Help us share the load.

When writing this book, I felt like there was something missing. At one point early in the writing process, I was talking to my younger brother, trying to convince him to join a climate group. My little brother has a huge heart and I'm really proud of the man he has become, but I still wish that he, like so many others, could go from caring about and supporting social movements from afar to being an active part of them.

As someone who knows him well, I got quite frustrated with the reasons he gave as to why he wasn't going to join a movement now: too little time, a lack of desire to join and many other reasons. Then, he said something that has stuck with me ever since: 'Why would I want to be a climate activist when I just see you hitting burnout all the time and constantly stressed. I don't want to be like that.' It felt like a blow to my stomach. Was this the picture that I was giving my loved ones of what it's like to be in movements? No wonder they didn't want to be involved.

There is often a misrepresentation of taking climate action as if the choice we have is between carrying on as normal or taking action that will mean we have to sacrifice the things we love. The reality is that if we don't do anything at all then things *will* get significantly worse. Simultaneously, as I hope you now know after reading this book, we have such a huge chance at making the world a better place if we take action now. Building this better world does not mean we have to let go of everything that we love and that brings us joy. Activism includes so much more than just sacrifice; there is also a huge amount of joy that this work can bring to our lives right now, through friendships and connections to each other. I know that, for me, the community I have found through climate-justice activism has made my world so much bigger and brighter than it was before.

Of course, I'm fighting to stop the bad things. I'm fighting to save lives. I'm fighting for every single person to be able to live in dignity. I'm fighting because I truly believe that once your eyes are open to the violence that exists in this world and is so painfully normalised, there is no other reasonable thing to do with your life but to try and change the world as much as you can for the better.

But I'm also fighting for the dreams of every single person who has not been allowed to dream. Every person that the oppressive systems of this world have weighed on so heavily. I'm fighting for a world in which everyone can pursue their dreams; where everyone can laugh, be silly, find joy, be creative and express their authenticity.

Imagine how many more people would want to take action if our movements looked healthier and more joyful? As adrienne maree brown says in their book *Pleasure Activism: The Politics of Feeling Good*, we need to make movements that people want to move towards. Being in competition with each other over who is more stressed or who is sacrificing more just pushes many people away from joining too. Let's create pockets of the liberated world we are fighting for now.

In getting to that world, we not only deserve to have joy ourselves now – we *need* to. This is not to say that the fight will be easy. It is not an invitation to put on rose-tinted glasses. We must still keep our eyes open and our hearts soft to the realities of this world. This is all still a struggle of course, but that does not mean that we all have to enforce miserable lives on ourselves. That misery does not help tackle oppression, it does not honour those who are forced into suffering, it just makes it harder for you to fight for the long run. In the same way, to have joy does not disrespect the often bleak and grim realities of this world, it just allows you to have the energy and the will to keep going.

We must remember that there are a small number of people whose best interests are for each and every one of us to lose hope in a better world. A very small percentage of the population – who profit from climate destruction and the oppression of the majority – want you to feel like your work isn't important, that life is just miserable and that nothing will ever change. To find joy is to affirm your own humanity. To find joy is to fill your soul, feed your imagination and navigate a way out of the darkness that surrounds us. To find joy is a powerful, essential tool for sustained resistance.

To choose to dance on dry lands rather than collapse is how we will survive every manifestation of apocalypse. To do both is how we remain human.

I want to be fighting for a better world for the rest of my time on this earth and I am hopeful that you do too.[********] If we're lucky, that should be quite a while yet. In order to do that, we need to be healthy along the way. We need to be part of a loving community. We need to be plugged into a movement of people who will encourage, challenge and hold us. We need to fall in love and hold our friends' hands, kiss their faces and laugh until our stomachs hurt. We need to run around in nature, roll in the grass, hug a tree, boogie in the kitchen, cry in wonder at how beautiful the evening sky looks and swim in the ocean. As someone with a complex and messy brain, I need to live a life that feels like it's worth fighting for.

******** It's not that this is what I'd genuinely want to be doing with my life – if we lived in a liberated world, then I'd probably spend all day scuba diving . . .

I used to believe that allowing myself these seemingly frivolous things disrespected the sacrifices of the many who came before me and fought for my liberation. Now I see it differently. I don't think my enslaved ancestors' wildest dreams were that I would spend my whole life being miserable, beating myself up for never doing enough and burning out constantly. I feel in my bones that my ancestors' wildest dreams would have been that I would fight for liberation whilst there is breath in my lungs and that I would also use that breath to laugh, to make deep declarations of love, squeal with joy, sing with my whole chest and give thanks for our continued presence on this earth. In a world that wants to grind me down, that wants us to burn out, our joy is an act of beautiful rebellion.

An important part of our hope is our ability to imagine. As I've mentioned a few times before, our radical imaginations are so deeply powerful. To have active hope, we need to be able to envisage what it is that we are running towards, as well as what we are running away from. We have to imagine what this new world will look like. We have to imagine something so exciting that we cannot help but do all we can to get there.

So, I want to give you a space to do that here. Imagine what the best world ever could be. Go all the way. Remember that the best, most liberated and joyful world you can imagine right now isn't even as good as it gets. Don't hold back. Don't be constrained by what might be realistic or achievable. Often, 'realistic' is another way of discouraging us from holding our heads up too high; of preventing us from challenging the ways of the world. We cannot accept oppression, exploitation or violence. We *have* to imagine more.

I would love for you to take a few minutes to write down in the space below what this future looks like for you – bullet points, full prose, whatever works for you. Just free-flow write it as it comes to you. When you're done – if this is your own copy, of course – I'd encourage you to rip out this page and stick it somewhere you'll see it often. Somewhere you will be reminded often of what you're fighting for. I hope this will keep you in the movement for the long run and remind you that whilst this book began being written by me, climate justice is a living movement that must be written by all of us.

This fight cannot only be worth it if we are guaranteed to completely win the new world within our lifetimes. Make no mistake, what we are fighting for is huge. It's unlikely to be won completely within my lifetime. We might not even be able to see the changes happening around us. That does not mean we give up. That does not mean the fight is not worth it. There is so much we won't see. There is so much we haven't seen. For so many of us, the degree to which we are liberated is the result of so many actions – big and small – of those who came before us. I am so glad that they thought acting to change the world was worth it. I might not be here if they hadn't.

Every action we take will contribute to the movement, whether you see it or not. It will contribute to inevitable tipping points. The more people we have actively working towards a better world, the sooner we'll get there. Every fraction of a degree of warming that we can prevent matters. Every single fraction of a degree of warming is lives saved. Every action we take is so, so worth it.

So, don't just sit around hoping that someone else will come along and give you the hope you need, but start being a part of building that hope. Do what you're good at that can help us in creating that change and do it to the best of your ability. Join the millions of people who are transforming the world around us every single day. Hold on to these words by Octavia E. Butler from her novel *The Parable of the Sower*: 'All that you touch you Change. All that you Change Changes you. The only lasting truth is Change. God Is Change.'[99]

I truly believe – I *have* to believe – that we will win this fight eventually. It will be long, the struggle will be constant, but I believe deep in my soul that if enough of us fight for it, we will get a better world.

FURTHER READING

Max Ajl, *A People's Green New Deal* (2021, Pluto Press)

Naomi Klein, *This Changes Everything: Capitalism vs The Climate* (2014, Simon & Schuster)

Jason Hickel, *Less is More* (2020, Cornerstone)

Amelia Horgan, *Lost in Work* (2021, Pluto Press)

Tithi Bhattacharya, *Social Reproduction Theory* (2017, Pluto Press)

Aaron Vansintjan, Andrea Vetter and Matthias Schmelser, *The Future is Degrowth* (2022, Verso)

adrienne maree brown, *Emergent Strategy* (2017, AK Press)

Rebecca Solnit, *Hope in the Dark* (2016, Canongate Books)

Cradle Community, *Brick by Brick* (2021, Hajar Press)

Tori Tsui, *It's Not Just You* (2023, Simon & Schuster)

adrienne maree brown, *Pleasure Activism* (2019, AK Press)

Vanessa Nakate, *A Bigger Picture* (2021, Pan Macmillan)

Angela Davis, *Are Prisons Obsolete?* (2003, Seven Stories Press)

Angela Davis, *Freedom Is A Constant Struggle* (2016, Haymarket Books)

Olufemi O. Taiwo, *Elite Capture* (2022, Pluto Press)

BIBLIOGRAPHY

Introduction

* Audre Lorde, *Sister Outsider: Essays and Speeches* (Crossing Press, 1984; reprinted by Penguin Modern Classics, 2019)

1. What is Climate Justice?

* 'Climate Change and Health', *Lancet*, 2012, *Lancet*, 2015
* 'Sink or swim: How Indigenous and community lands can make or break nationally determined contributions', Forest Declaration Assessment (2022). https://forestdeclaration.org/wp-content/uploads/2022/03/Sink-or-swim-IPLC-lands-and-NDCs.pdf
* Max Ajl, *A People's Green New Deal* (Pluto Press, 2021)
* Audre Lorde, 'Learning from the 60s', speech at Malcolm X weekend, Harvard University, February 1982.
* Hilary Graham, *Unequal Lives: Health and Socioeconomic Inequalities* (Open University Press, 2006)

2. So Who's Responsible?

* IPCC report (most recent)
* Ayisha Siddiqa poem, performed at COP27
* Runnymede Trust and Greenpeace UK, 'Confronting Injustice: Racism and the Environmental Emergency Report' (2022),https://www.runnym edetrust.org publications/confronting-injustice-racism-and-the environmental-emergency
* Michael Parenti, (1986)
* Mary Eleanor Spear and John Tukey, Figure 5.1, refs 44-5.
* Daniel Ribeiro
* Olúfémi O. Táíwò, *Reconsidering Reparations* (OUP, 2022) https://tradingeconomics.com/pakistan external-debt #:~:text=External%20Debt%20in%20Pakistan%20

averaged,the%20third%20quarter%20of%202004.
* Debt Justice: https://debtjustice.org.uk/countries-in-crisis/debt-crisis-pakistan
* https://www.twn.my/title2/briefing_papers/post2020/UN_Biodiversity_meetings/Debt%20biodiversity%20TWNBP%20Dec%202022%20Gaster%20et%20al.pdf
* https://www.macrotrends.net/countries/NER/niger/population-growth-rate
* http://www.globalcarbonatlas.org/en/CO2-emissions
* F. Ibrahim, *Capitalism versus Planet Earth: An Irreconcilable Conflict*, vol. 1. (Muswell Press, 2012)
* (Vasquez del Aguila, 2016)
* https://digitalcommons.usf.edu/cgi/viewcontent.cgi?article=1740&context=gsp
* F. Akhter, 'The state of contraceptive technology in Bangladesh. Issues in Reproductive and Genetic Engineering', *Journal of International Feminist Analysis* (1988)., 1(2), pp.153–8.
* Michelle Chan,
* https://www.theguardian.com/world/commentisfree/2019/mar/20/eco-fascism-is-undergoing-a-revival-in-the-fetid-culture-of-the-extreme-right
* https://earth.org/what-is-ecofascism/
* Naomi Klein, *This Changes Everything* (Penguin, 2015)

3. Beyond White Environmentalism

* Mary Annaise Heglar, 'Climate Change Isn't the First Existential Threat', (Zora, 2019)
* Max Ajl, *A People's Green New Deal* (Pluto Press, 2021)
* UN Special Rapporteur on Human Rights and the Environment, 'Sacrifice Zones: 50 of the Most Polluted Places on Earth'

* Runnymede and Greenpeace UK report, 2022
* Greenpeace UK, 2020
* Alexandra Wanjiku Kelbert, 'Confronting Injustice: Racism and the Environmental Emergency' (Report from Greenpeace and Runnymede Trust, 2022)
* https://qz.com/1226984/environmental-racism-has-left-black-americans-three-times-more-likely-to-die-from-pollution/
* Ayana Elizabeth Johnson, 'I'm a Black climate expert. Racism derails our efforts to save the planet', *Washington Post* (June 2020).
* Friends of The Earth Europe, 2013
* https://www.euronews.com/green/2020/07/20/the-dark-side-of-forest-conservation-the-sengwer-tribe-and-embobut-forest
* https://www.opendemocracy.net/en/north-africa-west-asia/how-palestines-climate-apartheid-is-being-depoliticised/
* 'NOT-ZERO: How "net zero" targets disguise climate inaction, Joint technical briefing by climate justice organizations', 2020
* Leo Cerda

4. Deconstructing Capitalism

* Author's Q&A on Instagram
* Jason Hickel, 'Less Is More' Talk at Advaya Event, Economics of Happiness: Post-Growth, Localisation and Wellbeing, 20 June 2017
* Emma Dabiri, *What White People Can Do Next: From Allyship to Coalition* (Penguin, 2021)
* The Prison Industrial Complex: Mapping Private Sector Players, 2018
* https://www.prisonpolicy.org/blog/2017/04/10/wages/

- * Hickel J, Sullivan D, Zoomkawala H. Rich countries drained $152tn from the Global South since 1960. In: Al Jaseera [Internet]. 6 May 2021 [cited 5 Aug 2022]. Available: https://www.aljaseera.com/opinions/2021/5/6/rich-countries-drained-152tn-from-the-global-south-since-1960
- * Naomi Klein, *This Changes Everything* (Penguin, 2015)
- * Ursula Le Guin
- * Ruth Wilson-Gilmore, https://mobile.twitter.com/CaseyGrants/status/1600128662795595777
- * Angela Y. Davis, 'How Does Change Happen', Lecture at U.C. Davis, 2007.
- * Octavia E. Butler, *The Parable of The Sower* (Headline, 2019).

5. In Denial Much? The Fossil-fuel Industry

Ed Garvey, in an interview on Drilled: A True Crime Podcast About Climate Change with Amy Westervelt

- * https://climatecommunication.yale.edu/publications/climate-change-in-the-american-mind-april-2019/toc/2/
- * Lauren MacDonald, speaking at 'Decarbonising Fossil Fuels' panel, TED Countdown, Edinburgh, 20xx.
- * Ibid.
- * https://e360.yale.edu/digest fossil-fuels-received-5-9-trillion-in-subsidies-in-2020-report-finds#:~:text=Fossil%20Fuels%20Received%20%245.9%20Trillion%20In%20Subsidies%20in%202020%2C%20Report%20Finds,-An%20open%2Dpit&text=Coal%2C%20oil%2C%20and%20natural%20gas,from%20the%20International%20Monetary%20Fund.
- * https://www.amnesty.org/en/latest/news/2017/06 shell-

complicit-arbitrary-executions-ogoni-nine-writ-dutch-court/
* https://waronwant.org/news-analysis/bad-company-bp-human-rights-and-corporate-crimes
* https://www.amnestyusa.org/chevron-found-guilty-in-8-billion-ecuadorian-human-rights-and-environmental-case/#:~:text=After%20an%20eighteen%2Dyear%2C%20multinational,sensitive%20part%20of%20the%20rainforest.
* https://www.amisdelaterre.org/communique-presse/a-nightmare-named-total-in-uganda-new-report-reveals-extent-of-violations-by-french-oil-major-on-the-eve-of-the-appeal-court-judgement-in-duty-of-vigilance-case/
* Climate Justice Alliance
* Kwasi Kwarteng, Twitter
* https://renewableenergy.usask.ca/news-articles/the-benefits-of-community-owned-renewable-energy-projects.php#:~:text=In%20summary%2C%20the%20key%20benefits,money%20for%20other%20community%20needs
* https://www.wearepossible.org/energy-local

6. Too Radical or Not Radical Enough?

* UN Secretary-General António Guterres, at press conference launching IPPC report, 28 February 2022.
* Aurora Levins Morales, 'Bigger is Better in Medicine Stories: Essays for Radicals', (Duke University Press Books; revised edition 2019).
* Audre Lorde, 'The Master's Tools Will Never Dismantle the Master's House', (Penguin Modern Paperback, 2018).
* André Gorz, Strategy for Labour, 1968
* Aurora Levins Morales, 'Bigger Is Better' (as above)

7. You Don't Know What You Don't Know

* Tariq Ali, *Winston Churchill: His Times, His Crimes* (Verso, 2022)
* Rynnstar, @therealrynnstar
* Jacob V. Joyce
* Fopé Ajanaku
* Farzana Khan, *New Constellations* podcast
* Jess Mally, speaking on *The YIKES Podcast*
* Olufemi Taiwo, *Elite Capture*, (Pluto Press, 2021)
* adrienne maree brown, *We Will Not Cancel Us* (AK Press, 2021)
* bell hooks, in conversation with Maya Angelou, 1998
* adrienne maree brown, *We Will Not Cancel Us* (as above).

8. That's Not the Type of Diversity We Want

* Emma Dabiri, *What White People Can Do Next* (Penguin 2021).
* Aurora Levins Morales, 'Class, Privilege and Loss', *Medicine Stories* (Duke University Press Books; revised edition 2019)
* https://twitter.com/emmadesaram/status/1526141626208354304
* Shaista Aziz
* Rishi Sunak.

9. Heroes Won't Save Us, But Community Will

Andre Henry

* Alicia Garza, *The Purpose of Power (Black Swan, 2021).*
* Rachel Chavkin, acceptance speech, Tony Awards, 6 August 2019.
* Ash Sarkar, 'Dump Him' Feminism Isn't Revolutionary. It's Callous' Novara Media, September 2022.

* Alicia Garza, *The Purpose of Power* (as above).
* Ibid.
* Fellow SNCC Activist on Ella Baker
* Arundhati Roy, War Talk (South End Press, 2003).
* adrienne maree brown, *Emergent Strategy: Shaping Change, Changing Worlds (AK Press, 2019)*

10. Hope as an Active Stance

* Mary Annaise Heglar
* Octavia E. Butler, *The Parable of the Sower*, (Octavia E. Butler, The Parable of The Sower (Headline, 2019).

ACKNOWLEDGEMENTS

Where to begin! I want to first thank you for picking up this book and reading it. That truly means so much to me. I hope that you're more than ready to begin or continue organising for climate justice now.

This book has been shaped by all the people I have had the pleasure of acting alongside in this flight. It is my love letter to each and every one of you – I am so grateful for the passion, energy and sacrifice you put into creating a better world for us all, whether it is seen or unseen. I am so deeply grateful for you all. The world would be a much worse place without all of your work.

Now for some people who I absolutely must thank by name.

I have to start with my family. To my parents Alcia and Mark – thank you both for always encouraging me to fight for justice, challenge what seems currently impossible and to never give up in the face of sometimes overwhelming adversity.

Mum, you are one of the most empathetic people I have ever met, and you passed your huge heart onto me. You were the first to teach me that feeling things intensely is a strength, and the natural way we should respond to injustice in this world.

Dad, when I said I cared about an issue, you would always challenge me to actually do something about it. It was that encouragement that has brought me to where I am today, and I will forever be grateful to you for that.

Josh, thank you for believing that I could write a book from the start. I appreciate you, little bro.

I began seriously writing this book in Jamaica, after conversations with my grandma. Grandma, thank you for encouraging me to laugh and find joy during this long process.

I would not have even been able to be in Jamaica – let alone been able to write this book – if it wasn't for the encouragement of my medical school mentor, Dr Sonia. Dr Sonia, thank you for believing me when I really needed you to as a fellow Black woman in medicine, and pushing me to follow my calling and take care of my wellbeing. Taking a sabbatical from medical school is one of the most important things I've ever done, and I wouldn't have done it if it wasn't for your help. I will forever be grateful to you.

To the team who actually brought this book from my mind and into the world – my sensational, passionate literary agent Kemi Ogunsanwo, whose persistence, belief, energy and support moved me from talking about writing a book to actually doing it. Thank you for listening to my long, meandering voice notes in wobbly times, and always meeting me where I'm at with kindness and encouragement. I am so deeply grateful to have you in my corner – you're amazing!

Marleigh Price, my brilliant editor at DK who shaped this book so beautifully and was always there to talk me away from overthinking or spiralling, it was such an honour to work with you on this book. Your heart really comes through in all the work you do.

To the rest of the wonderful team at DK: Silvia Dembner, Cora Siedlecka, Katie Cowan, Issy Panay, Hayley Scaife, Helen Poultney, Amy Pearson, Izzy Holton, Amy Cox and Maxine Pedliham – thank you so much for all the work you've done to bring this book to life and into the world. Thanks to Holy Moly UK for designing this brilliantly eye-catching book cover.

I also have to mention here my brilliant manager Adam, and all the SHFT team for how much they have supported and believed in my work daily over the years – you're the best!

To the brilliant, huge-hearted Layla F Saad for your encouragement and for talking me through the world of publishing to make it all a little less opaque and scary.

Unending thanks to my chosen family and first-readers of chapters in this book: Rhiannon Osborne, Jess Mally, Jo Becker, Tom Allen-Olivar and Lauren MacDonald. Your comments, thoughts and help were so insightful, and have really made this book what it is today. You're all absolutely incredible people and my respect and love for you has no bounds.

To Daisy, for being the fellow nerdy book-worm I needed as a kid. I probably wouldn't have fallen in love with reading and writing as deeply if not for our friendship. I'm excited for when we will also be celebrating your book!

To Mr Firth and Mr Thomas for being great English teachers, and pushing me to pursue my love for writing alongside my medical career.

To Tori, Domi, Momo and Ella for being the supportive pals I dreamed of having as a kid.

To my T, thank you for supporting me every single step of the way with this book, in all my work and in life. Your unending support in a hard time in my life made writing this book possible. I couldn't have done so much of this without your never-ceasing support and love. There are no words I could write to encompass my gratitude to be doing life with you.

Finally, of course, all glory to God. I'm grateful for the path the Divine has guided me on so far and I am excited for whatever that looks like next.